THE GREAT GARAGE SALE BOOK

How to Run a Garage, Tag, Attic, Barn, or Yard Sale

SYLVIA SIMMONS

AN AUTHORS GUILD BACKINPRINT.COM EDITION

The Great Garage Sale Book:
How to Run a Garage, Tag, Attic, Barn or Yard Sale
All Rights Reserved © 1981, 2000 by Sylvia Simmons

AN AUTHORS GUILD BACKINPRINT.COM EDITION

Published by iUniverse.com, Inc.

For information address:
iUniverse.com, Inc.
620 North 48th Street, Suite 201
Lincoln, NE 68504-3467
www.iuniverse.com

Originally published by Contemporary Books, Inc.

ISBN: 0-595-08957-7

Printed in the United States of America

for
Hans
my partner in all things

FOREWORD

There's no doubt about it. Garage sales are now one of the favorite weekend participatory sports in the U.S.A. They are also a source of ready income for folks cleaning out their houses, preparing to move, liquidating an estate, or just turning over a new lifestyle leaf and getting rid of ancestral *junque* at the same time.

For everyone who has a hankering to join the nouveau riche of the Garage Sale Circuit, this *Great Garage Sale Book* is an ideal how-to guide. Within these pages, you will learn how to plan for and schedule your sale, how to select and price the merchandise, and how to keep friendly control over the customers. I have included advice and examples of advertising, promotion and display techniques. You will also find some practical tips on how to handle and protect your money at garage sale time and whether or not you should combine your sale with a partner.

You will find a lot of fun and humor mixed in with the good business suggestions. Practical garage sale case histories illustrate the do's and don'ts of the trade. And there is a special chapter on running an apartment-dweller's version of the garage sale, *plus* an instructive commentary on how to shop someone else's sale.

Now, for some money-making advice…

Sylvia Simmons

Contents

1

The Name of the Game Doesn't Matter: It's How You Play It That Pays Off

A garage sale by any other name can reap rich rewards just as readily as one that is tagged a garage sale. It's the game that matters, not the name.

In the Midwest, selling anything from a hodgepodge of bric-a-brac to a full household of exquisite furnishings is usually called a garage sale. In Connecticut and Massachusetts, the same type of event is known as a tag sale. Farther north in New England, in Vermont and New Hampshire, they are known as barn sales. In the Southwest, these enterprises are called backyard sales or white elephant sales. On the West Coast I have seen them promoted as flea markets, though in the East a flea market is a term used to designate a temporary and fairly large marketplace set up by a large number of sellers (often antique dealers) to which the public is invited. I have also known people to publicize their events as junk sales, thus giving the impression that the merchandise will be both cheap and inexpensive. In some areas, terms like attic sale and yard sale are used commonly. In urban areas, they may be dubbed loft sales, apartment sales, or stoop sales, which are growing in popularity.

The name of the game doesn't matter. *The one you should select is the one that is most often used in your area.* This makes it unnecessary for you to explain in your advertising or on your signs what kind of a happening you're conducting. By now this sort of activity is well-known just about everywhere, having grown by leaps and bounds in the last decade. So your local or regional designation is probably familiar to you.

For the purpose of simplification and brevity, and because it's the term most commonly used and generally understood, I'm going to use the name garage sale in this book. But all the information and advice included here applies to any such sale, regardless of its handle.

I will also speak of the ordinary household garage sale to differentiate the sort of event you're likely to sponsor from the highly specialized types of sales run by dealers, home liquidators, and auctioneers.

Just remember that it isn't the name of the game but how well you play it, and how carefully you follow the rules, that will determine how successfully you turn your rags into riches.

Now, for some money-making advice.

2

What's in It for You?

There are three principal reasons why people run garage sales: to get rid of a lot of possessions they no longer need or want, to make some money, and to have a great adventure. Most people will tell you that their aim is to dispose of a lot of things they no longer use or enjoy owning. But whatever *your* primary motivation for considering such a sale, chances are you will succeed in all three objectives if you plan and conduct it in a knowledgeable and sophisticated manner.

Deciding What You Want to Get Out of Your Sale

No one really gets wildly rich on a garage sale, though people who are disposing of the contents of an entire home or apartment and those with valuable antiques will usually realize a handsome sum from the proceeds. Ordinarily, however, anyone with a sizable estate to liquidate, particularly if valuable antiques or paintings are involved, will not

3

take the garage sale route but will call in an appraiser, an auction house, or a reputable dealer in antiques and let such specialists buy outright or otherwise handle disposal of the merchandise. This book is not about such sales, which are of a totally different nature from the ordinary household garage sale. While the ordinary garage sale doesn't make anyone fabulously wealthy, it can make you a bit richer than you were before.

Two Ways to Think about Your Sale

Whatever your number one objective, it is essential—even before you set the date—that you develop a personal philosophy about the proceeds of your sale. You must decide (1) whether you will want to get a specific cash amount for each item you plan to sell, and withdraw items from the sale if they fail to realize that specified amount or (2) whether you will be happy to settle for a total dollar amount on the full lot of the sale items, without worrying about how little you get for any specific item.

I strongly recommend Plan 2, but it's your property and your sale, so *you* have to make the choice. If you put a price on each item and hold fast to that price because you think it's worth what you're asking and you don't want to give it away, you may be left with a number of unsold pieces. Your attic, garage, or basement won't be totally cleaned out, though it may look a lot better after the sale than before it. Of course, under these circumstances, you won't suffer any regrets about having parted with something for less than the value you place on it.

Plan 2 offers different pluses and minuses. If you put extremely low prices on most items, they will probably be snapped up right away because there are a lot of people who can't resist a real bargain when they come across one. Keep in mind that garage sale shoppers come in two varieties: those who are seeking some specific things, such as secondhand furniture or secondhand children's clothes; and those who go to browse in the hope of finding an irresistible bargain. You probably know from your own experience, if you have patronized garage sales, that it's not unusual to walk out with something you don't really need and hadn't planned to buy but bought because the price was so low you felt it was virtually a giveaway.

The principal advantage of very low prices, which are usually cut even lower on the last day of the sale (more on this in Chapter 19), is that you will probably dispose of almost all the sale items and end up with a tidy sum for the lot, as well as the cleanest house on the block. But it takes a strong will and a predetermined philosophy to go this route. You cannot look backward when the sale is over and tell yourself, "I bet I could have gotten twice that price for my pewter ashtray! I was really silly to mark it so low." Don't fret. There is no guarantee that you would have found a willing customer at the higher price. And, after all, your objective was to dispose of it by turning it into cash, wasn't it? And you accomplished that, didn't you?

So make peace with either of the philosophies you pick. *But be certain, if you have a spouse or housemate who owns half the merchandise up for sale, that he or she shares your philosophy.* Nothing can spoil the fun of the whole experience more than a partner who taunts you (or himself or herself) with regrets about what might have been. Done is done.

And gone is gone You can't undo the sale once it's over, so if you have any doubts at all about whether you want to part with an item forever, don't include it. What you can do is place all of your "undecided" items in a corner of your house and have some blank tags handy. Sometimes a sale is going so well and you get so excited about the speed with which items are moving out, that you may choose to put some or all of the "undecided" items up for sale, perhaps with prices that are high enough so that, should they sell, you will have no regrets. Also, people often ask for a specific item and, if you have that particular thing tucked away, you should be prepared to say, "I do have one, but I'm not certain about selling it. I'll let you look at it so you can see if it's what you had in mind. But I must tell you in advance that if I do decide to sell it I'm going to want X dollars for it." Almost nothing whets the appetite more than an item that is hard to come by—and an eager buyer is much more likely to pay you a handsome price.

Once you have made up your mind which sale philosophy you're going to adopt, be sure you can live with it comfortably. Then be certain you can get the support of the other person or persons involved in the sale. As soon as these points are settled you're ready to get going.

3

Choosing the Best Time to Run Your Sale

The best time for a garage sale is when you have tons of great merchandise that you would like to unload, when there are hundreds of people in your area looking for bargains, when the weather is superb in every way, and when money is plentiful in your community.

That, of course, is the optimum time for a sale. But don't sit around waiting for just those circumstances. They're not likely to come all at once and, if you procrastinate, you may never get rid of all that stuff in your home.

From a realistic standpoint the best time to run a garage sale is when you have a sufficient number of items you want to dispose of and when you can see your way clear to make the time, over a period of two or three weeks, to do the preparatory planning and plotting for such an event. As to the weather, well, good weather is preferable to bad weather and, obviously, outdoor sales in midwinter don't attract as many people as those held on springlike or autumn days.

Your own good sense and the weather patterns for the region in which you live will suggest the best times of year. Generally speaking, May through October is the best sale period, unless you live in a part of the country where you can expect uncomfortably hot weather or frequent rains during any of those months. I have, however, run some fantastically successful sales in bad weather, including one in an apartment house that took place when there was almost a foot of snow outdoors and many people were staying home from work. Frequently, a rainy day will bring out people who might otherwise be playing golf or going to the beach. Keep in mind, of course, that inclement weather means no merchandise outside. Everything moves into the garage and toolshed or into a single room you've set aside for this activity.

The Best Days and Hours

The best sale days are Friday, Saturday, and Sunday. If you plan a two-day event, Saturday and Sunday usually yield the greatest return. If you prefer not to do business on Sunday, a Friday–Saturday sale will allow you the two-day spread that works to your advantage and includes one day when most working people in your neighborhood will be free to browse.

The best hours are from 9:00 a.m. or 10:00 a.m. to sundown. You want to allow enough time before darkness falls to move your merchandise indoors. Of course, if your sale is to be in an apartment, there is no reason why you can't let it continue into the early evening to catch working people who might not be getting home before 6:00 or 7:00 p.m. But, generally speaking, a sale that goes from 10:00 a.m. to 4:00 p.m. for two days will result in almost as many transactions as one that runs from 9:00 to 6:00, particularly if you include at least one day that is a Saturday, a Sunday, or a holiday.

Naturally, it's nice if you can be flexible enough so that, should you get a last surge of traffic just about closing time on your first day, you can remain open until the traffic eases off. If you follow the advice in Chapter 17, which discusses your social life during your garage sale evenings, you're not likely to be going out anyway, and the extra dollars you might make in those late-hour transactions will justify your delay in putting up the "CLOSED" sign.

4

How to Select Your Sale Merchandise

Selection of merchandise for your garage sale should be based on the layaway plan and should never be done at the last minute.

The time to start selecting and laying aside the things you are going to sell is the first moment that the idea of having a garage sale occurs to you. You may make that decision in midwinter and plan the sale for midsummer, but that doesn't mean you should wait until summer to lay aside the merchandise you hope to dispose of.

Even if, when you first decide to have a sale, you can think of only a few disposables offhand—a handful of garments, a boxful of toys, or some old mismatched dishes and glasses—it's never too soon to start your layaway program.

The first thing you should do is determine which room or closet in the house is going to be used to store the sale stuff. Believe me, whatever area you pick, it is not going to be big enough as time goes on, but at least you'll be able to make a start. So tell yourself that from now until sale time this

10

room, closet, part of the basement, or half of the attic—whatever—is going to look like a junk shop for some weeks or months. For that reason, because it *will* look simply awful for some time, pick the area most remote from the part of the house in which you entertain. You don't want to have to explain what the mess is all about every time someone visits you.

Then, whenever you come across something that you think you would like to include in your inventory, take it from its resting place and move it to the chosen spot. Obviously, this doesn't apply to furniture and large appliances or other big and bulky things that have to stay put until the first day of the big event. But the purpose of having a specific storage area for things you are going to dispose of is to give you an idea of how much you actually have (it's going to be more than you first thought), and to help you avoid overlooking an item as you get closer to the sale and are wrapped up in many of its details. When you are busy and preoccupied, it is quite possible to forget about a particular garment, or small kitchen gadgets, or even large items if they've been tucked away for years in an attic or toolshed.

This, of course, is a rather haphazard system of accumulating goods. You are also going to want a more systematic way of keeping track of your inventory. You'll need several boxes of different sizes. One or two of them can be quite small, preferably with covers, to hold old jewelry and other tiny possessions. At least one, to start with, should be rather large so that you can begin collecting toys, sporting goods, camera equipment, games, desk or office materials, and so on. Books and records can be stacked on the floor. Dresses and suits should be kept on their hangers until the sale, but sweaters, children's clothing, slacks, and blouses can be neatly folded and stacked.

Systematically Combing the House

When I run one of my own sales, I like to set aside a few hours each week to go through one room at a time, searching for things that have outlived their usefulness. I always start with the bedroom because it's relatively easy to go through the dresser drawers and closets and unearth a lot of goodies, some of which I had forgotten I owned because they were tucked away in the back. And I can usually do the living room in quick time, too, except for the bookshelves, which always produce treasures but which take me forever because I am inclined to stop and read old flyleafs and inscriptions and authors' biographies.

I save the attic for a day when I have no special plans and plenty of time. The same is true of the basement. And that is one arena where everyone in the family gets into the act, because we store a good deal of out-of-season possessions there—our lawn mowers and hoses in the winter and our leaf blower and snow thrower in the summer, among other things—and many of those items are not used by me but by others in the family who should have the privilege of deciding whether to sell them and buy some new equipment, or hang on to the old stuff for another year.

If there are children in your family, allow plenty of time to go through their clothes and possessions—*with them*. Most youngsters take a lot of time to decide whether to get rid of an old sled or some book they haven't glanced at in five years or a favorite ski sweater that has been outgrown. *Warning:* Don't, I repeat, *don't* assume, because you are the one who bought and paid for an item and will buy and pay for its replacement, that you have the right to determine whether to unload it in a garage sale. Better have that conference, even though it's going to eat up a lot of valuable time. Failure to do so can lead to a lot of stony silence when you ask for help from family members around sale time.

For most people, the kitchen is almost always a treasure trove. I like to go through that room when there's no one home and I'm not scheduled to prepare dinner. I take my time and systematically go through every drawer, every cupboard, every near-the-ceiling storage area. *And as I go, I clean!* I empty the flatware trays, pick out the items I want to get rid of, wash the trays, and neatly replace what I plan to keep. I remove all the pots and pans from the cabinets, sort them, separate them into "keep" and "dispose" piles and rearrange them so neatly that one would think we had just moved in. For those kitchen drawers that are lined I either wash the linings or replace them. Once I get into this cleanup spirit I usually go ahead and do the kitchen windows on the same day. When I've completed my thorough exploration of this room, my kitchen is unquestionably the cleanest one on the block—probably the cleanest on *anybody's* block. And yours will be, too!

My linen closet is another source of unexpected treasures. I always come across those pot holders and cute dish towels that seem to show up regularly as house gifts and that I rarely use because I'm nuts on the subject of my pot holders and dish towels matching the color scheme in my kitchen. Those that arrive with house guests always seem to be the wrong colors. My garage sale events also alert me to which bath towels are ready to be replaced and which bathroom might do with a new shower curtain, a new scale, or even a whole new color scheme. Knowing that I'm going to make some money by unloading the old stuff makes me feel less guilty about redoing a bathroom that could really serve, as is, for another year or so.

What homemaker hasn't squirreled away an old bedspread from the previous house or apartment—a spread that is fading away in disuse because it has been replaced by a new one that fits the new bedroom or guestroom decor? And what about those curtains from your last home, which will someday be cut and resewn to fit heaven-knows-which-windows? Since all the windows in the new place were long ago fitted with more suitable curtains, the old ones are better off in the sale where some enthusiastic browser will turn these rags into unexpected riches for you.

Making Your Merchandise Look Desirable

One more advantage of starting your layaway program well in advance of your sale is that it gives you adequate time to make certain items look better than when you unearthed them. Make a special pile of those things that need to be laundered or have buttons replaced. Pick a rainy day and clean and polish those tarnished items that have the potential for looking better.

If you're going to sell an old copper teakettle, shining it up will certainly increase the price you can ask for it. If you have an old radio for sale, put some new batteries in it to improve its performance; it will add more to the price you can ask than the cost of the batteries. Should you choose to sell some brass item, polishing and buffing it may take a bit of time but can sometimes as much as double the price you will be able to ask—and get. The problem is that once you put it back into nifty condition you may not want to sell it!

While it is true that some people equate a dirty old item with a cheap find, and while they have visions of taking it home and making it look like a million dollars, the general rule is that merchandise that looks like it has been cared for, and thus looks valuable, can command a higher price. So clean it up, dust it off, wash the glass, put in a new light bulb or battery, give it some spit and polish, and these items will find new homes quicker than you might have expected.

Getting the Family into the Act

When you begin to accumulate sale goods, explain what you're doing to everyone who lives in the house. Otherwise, you may find someone scattering your carefully stacked merchandise in search of a lost sneaker, or dumping coats or gloves or skates on top of the pile. Suggest that all hands give some thought to things in their own rooms, possessions that have outlived their usefulness, and ask that they place items they want to sell in the designated sale storage area.

All of you will find that, as you go about your daily business, you will spot items you would like to get rid of. The merchandise will mount, and you'll start to have some idea of how many tags you're going to need to mark all this stuff.

Let's talk about the tagging process next.

5

Tagging and Marking

I have been to garage sales at which most of the merchandise wasn't marked and people had to ask about the prices. I do not recommend this procedure at all. True, it could save you a good deal of time before the sale begins, but you have to realize that there are many people who are reluctant to ask about the price of an item unless they have already made up their minds to buy it—provided the price is right. These people sometimes feel that asking a price is making a commitment to buy, and they may not feel ready for such a commitment.

Thus, failure to put prices on the goods will discourage many a transaction. There is yet another reason for showing prices on merchandise: it urges the browser to scrutinize an item more closely and linger over it a little longer.

Occasionally, though happily not often, there is even a customer who thinks the lack of a price ticket is a device to "get what the traffic will bear." This creates an adversary relationship between potential buyer and seller and doesn't help consummate the sale.

Finally, if you have to tell every customer the price of every single item, it eats up a lot of your time once the sale is in progress—and a good deal of your energy, too. It also promotes errors, particularly if more than one person is managing or helping out at the event.

Two Ways to Tag

The two most common and useful ways to display your prices are with actual tags, which can be purchased in a variety of sizes at most stationery stores, and with ordinary masking tape. Masking tape is the least expensive and probably the quickest way to put prices on a large number of items, but it does have some drawbacks. Masking tape is excellent for glasses, crockery, garden tools, and hardy bric-a-brac. It is sometimes the only way to put a price on something that doesn't have a handle or a leg or some other projection for holding the string of a tag. But it doesn't work on clothing and shouldn't be used on fine furniture pieces where it might leave a mark after removal.

One of the advantages of using tags is that they are easy to spot, particularly on large items, and if the tag is big enough, it allows room for you to write or print a short legend that might encourage the potential purchaser to buy. This is important with merchandise whose higher prices might call for some justification: "Solid brass," "Circa 1920," "Original Little Orphan Annie mug," "Lining is hand-sewn," "Tablecloth is 102 inches by 30 inches," "Antique—one scratch on base, otherwise mint condition," "Comes apart for easy storage," etc. You can't very well do this sort of thing on masking tape. (See Chapter 8 for more information on legend copy.)

You can buy white, colored, or manila tags. The color isn't as important as the size. You don't want an enormous tag on a tiny item or vice versa. Nor do you want a tag so small that it's difficult to locate. As you accumulate your sale stock, you will get a good idea of how many small items and how many large ones are likely to need tags. I have found that the most useful sizes are 1½ inches by 2 inches, 1½ inches by 3¼ inches, and 3 inches by 5 inches for furniture and other large pieces.

In addition to masking tape and tags, I frequently use self-adhering stickers that can be purchased in small boxes or in sheets. Stickers that are 3 inches by 3 inches can be cut in two or in four to give you a variety of sizes, as needed.

Sometimes I buy a batch of colored tags, usually all the same color, and make that the color theme of my sale. I have used a nice bright green tag, light enough so that writing on it is legible, and have decorated my road signs with the same color. All my on-premise signs then pick up the green trim, which lends a professional air to the event and makes it look like a more important sale. Every little device you use to make your happening appear unusual or well thought out will enhance the proceedings and generate more customer traffic.

When you purchase your tags, also pick up some small safety pins. You will need them to pin your tags to any clothing or linens you plan to sell.

Of course, even more important than what the tags themselves look like is what they say. Your pricing philosophy and your legend copy will both become silent salesmen that can help you reap even greater profits than you had anticipated.

6

How to Set Your Prices

Once you have made up your mind to have a garage sale, pricing your goods will be the toughest part of the undertaking. You'll have fun planning the event and talking about it to your friends and neighbors. You'll probably enjoy the sale itself once the doors open and people start to come. When it is over you will entertain your friends for weeks with anecdotes about things that happened during this adventure. And if you're like most people, you'll get a kick out of turning a lot of things you *didn't* want into cash you *do* want so that you can purchase something that will give you or someone else more pleasure than a crowded attic or garage.

The only part of the whole proceedings you won't enjoy is figuring out what to charge for your merchandise. Many people hire garage sales consultants or professionals who will handle the whole sale for them just because they can't come to grips with the matter of deciding what things are worth, what they will bring when they are put up for sale, or which prices won't make them regret having sold the items at all. But hiring such consultants or garage sale brokers is expensive; they usually charge between a third and 40 percent of your gross take. It seems foolish to give away such a big part of your proceeds when you can really do it all yourself just by following the advice in this book and combining it with common sense and a willingness to do a bit of hard work over a fairly short period of time.

I talked earlier about developing a philosophy for your sale, about deciding whether you want to set a handsome price for each item (knowing that if you sold it for less you would be unhappy) or whether you want to mark most things so low that they virtually walk away, and quickly. Once you have picked a philosophy, the pricing step becomes less difficult. But I kid you not: it is never easy. So be prepared for a period of indecisiveness.

Begin Your Pricing Early

Here's how to get started. If at all possible, begin your pricing and tagging ten days or a week before your sale. Even that is just barely enough time; two weeks is even better. It is going to take you many more hours than you imagine it will. Perhaps more important, pricing things well in advance gives you a few days before you open your doors to the public during which you can change your mind and alter a price upward or downward. Sometimes, after pricing an item, you may feel so much regret at what you wrote on the ticket that you'll want to rip it up and write another. Conversely, you might decide that certain prices are too high and that your desire to be rid of the items is so strong for some reason—"they take too much space"; "they're an eyesore"; "I replaced it with a better one months ago"—that you would almost be glad to pay someone to take them away.

We once had an old pump in our basement, left over from a previous well that had been dug by the previous owner of the house. I longed to be free of the ugly monster. When our next garage sale came along I put a price tag of $5 on it. It was sold so fast I almost thought it had run off on its own ugly black stumps. To this day I believe someone who didn't know what it was grabbed it because it looked like it might be worth much more! Or maybe the buyer *did* know more than I—perhaps it could have been reconditioned and sold for a good deal more money. Whatever the case, I would have been happy to pay $5 to the refuse man to take it from the premises, but he didn't handle that sort of thing and had suggested I take it to the town dump—something I never got around to doing.

The point of this long, dreary tale is that, with an extremely low ticket, your eyesore can be made to disappear and you soon forget you ever owned it. You end up with a bit more free space and you have a few extra bucks in the kitty. All of which is to say that pricing takes some thinking and the more time you allow for it, the fewer regrets you're likely to have.

Tag as You Go

As you go through your house, attic, garage, and basement, through dresser drawers and closets—every area or cupboard where you might have things you would like to dispose of—carry with you a box of tags, pins, stickers, and masking tape that you will use in your pricing operation (see the list of supplies located in Chapter 22). Don't spend undue time with small items that aren't worth much. Come to a quick decision, for better or for worse, about old measuring cups, inexpensive garden tools, excess clothes hangers, and used towels (yes, people *do* buy used towels; they make excellent rags or a clean lining for the cat's basket) and spend more of your time and effort on bigger and more valuable items: furniture, sets of china, good clothing, appliances, pictures, antiques, lamps—the things a retailer would call "big ticket items."

How Much Should I Charge?

Here are the mental steps you should take, steps that will

become fairly automatic after a little experience. First, ask yourself what you originally paid for each item and how much use you got out of it. Then, determine whether you've used it in recent months and are likely to need it in the future or use it with any degree of frequency. Do you have a newer or better item of a similar or improved kind, one that means you will probably never go back to using this one? For example, if you have a black-and-white TV set that has been replaced by a color set, are you likely to go back to watching black and white, except when the color set is out for repairs?

Perhaps the most important question of all is this one: what would a potential buyer need to pay for a brand-new model of this item if he or she were to buy it in a store? Pursuing the example of the TV set, if you believe that someone could buy a black-and-white set in this make and size for $110, and get a guarantee with it, which you will not be offering, would that individual be willing to pay $89 for *your* set? The answer is a definite no. So, if you truly want to dispose of that set, you are going to have to make it such a bargain—perhaps $49—that someone will say to himself: "At that price, I'll take my chances. Maybe it will work well for a long time. And even if it should need minor repairs, I'd still come out with a saving. It's a gamble, but I'll take it because I haven't much to lose."

If the item you're about to price is not one that carries a guarantee at the store, then you have to engage in the same thinking along slightly different lines: "I have these ice skates. We never skate anymore. A new pair of adult skates runs about $50 nowadays. But we only paid $20 for them many years ago and we had lots of pleasure using them. I'd be delighted to trade them for a ten-dollar bill." The prospective buyer, in his or her turn, figures this way: "They probably need sharpening. That's $3. But at that price I'm still saving more than $25 and they look like good skates. I think it's a terrific buy. The leather is a bit scuffed, but new skates get that way in no time at all. They fit just fine and I'm going to take them."

If those skates had been priced at $20 on the assumption that a buyer would still be getting them for less than half what he might pay in the store, they might not have moved so rapidly, or at all. Keep in mind that you would have needed not only someone interested in ice skates but someone who also wears the same size as you. This narrows down the market considerably and means you need a really seductive price so that the rare perfect fit can't resist your rare perfect bargain.

There will be many instances in which you cannot base your price on what someone would have to pay for a similar item at a local retail store because the local store may not carry anything like it. This would apply to antiques, certain clothing, special pieces of furniture, an old rug, a home-grown houseplant, a painting, or some old but mint-condition records.

Let's take furniture as an example. While antique furniture commands very high prices these days (and if you have quite a few such antiques, you should probably call in an antique dealer to tell you what he would pay you for them), ordinary secondhand furniture brings next to nothing when sold to dealers. Only if you have a houseful of such old furniture to dispose of and want to avoid selling it by yourself should you consider the dealer route. Remember, the dealer has to make a profit, so he is going to mark up the price before selling the furniture. Therefore, he has to buy it for much less than the retail customer will be ready to pay. If the amount of furniture you want to get rid of is limited to a dozen or fewer pieces, you will do quite a bit better financially if you include them in your garage sale. True enough, you might have to negotiate a number of transactions rather than a single one with the dealer, but the difference in the prices you will get will be well worth your time.

Another possibility is to separate your furniture pieces from the other sale items and advertise them by themselves, even though all the merchandise will be sold on the same days. There are people who don't go to many garage sales but who might be interested in secondhand furniture for a second home or apartment and they might look in the classifieds under "Merchandise for Sale."

To price each piece of furniture, examine it with the eye of a stranger. How new (or how old) does it look? Is it badly scratched and in need of refinishing? Or is it in mint condition? If it is an upholstered piece, is it in need of an upholstering job, which can be very expensive? Is the fabric torn? Are the springs in good condition? Is it dirty or clean? Is it something that is likely to be used in a family room or playroom or is it suitable for an elegant living or dining room? All these factors determine what will be considered a reasonable price.

I recently ran an apartment sale with no advertising beyond circulars distributed to 300 families who lived in the building. I had a lovely contemporary sofa for sale. It was upholstered in a handsome striped beige in a tone that would fit into many color schemes. It was clean. But a young child who had visited us had jumped up and down on this piece before his parents could stop him and had broken one of the springs. We had paid approximately $600 for the sofa ten years earlier. A new sofa such as that, given inflation and today's prices, would cost in the neighborhood of $1,000. But we hadn't paid $1,000 for it and we had enjoyed it for a decade. We had, in fact, gotten all our money's worth out of it. If the right customer came along, I know I might have received at least $300 for that piece—it was worth every nickel of it. But my sale was to run a mere day and a half. After that, the apartment had to be vacated for a new tenant. If I didn't sell the sofa and had to move it by truck to our other residence, where I already had three sofas and no need or room for another, it would cost money and would be a large nuisance. That sofa simply had to go. So I tagged it at $149, and it sold quickly. I must confess I felt a momentary pang of regret when the third person to arrive at the sale walked right to the sofa, looked at the price, sought me out, and said, "I want that sofa." But I leaned heavily on my sale philosophy, not to worry about what might have been, and pocketed the purchaser's check. Gone is gone.

Pricing Secondhand Garments

Just plain old clothes are not easy to sell. If what you have is worn, out of style, or has no special appeal, you might be better off donating them to Goodwill Industries, the Salvation Army, the Hadassah, your local thrift shop, or any charity that sells secondhand clothing. Any of these organizations will give you a card or letter stating their evaluation of the merchandise you have donated. Not only does the giving of charity make you feel good, but it's tax-deductible.

On the other hand, if you do want to turn your rags into riches, certain items can bring fairly good prices. Those that move well at garage sales include things in near-new condition, clothing with designer names on the labels, outgrown but serviceable children's garments, kicky items like a worn-out fur coat or an outmoded evening gown (teenagers often squeal in delight when they see these), shoes never or hardly ever worn because they turned out to fit poorly, and good-quality men's or women's suits that you have to dispose of because of weight gains or losses. New clothing is so expensive these days, particularly designer clothes and outerwear that people who might not, in previous years, have considered wearing someone else's garments are sometimes willing to consider doing so.

Pricing clothing is something you almost have to do blindfolded. How much space does it take in the closet? When was the last time it was worn? Does it still fit? Does it annoy you to open the door of a crowded closet and realize that you are giving rent-free space to a number of items that have outlived their usefulness? When you have thought hard about each item, pin a tag to the sleeve and write on it whatever you believe would be a good token price, just enough so you won't feel you're giving it away for nothing. You will be surprised at how these so-called token prices add up. You might, for example, price a couple of men's suits at $20 each; after all, they are worth nothing to your husband if he won't or can't wear them anymore. A couple of pairs of almost-new shoes could be priced at $10 a pair, but keep in mind that you won't be able to sell old, worn-out shoes at *any* price. A heavy outer coat and a cape you never should have bought in the first place could be marked at $25 each. A half-dozen blouses could be priced at $4 each; a woman's designer-name suit, with label intact, at $35; three pairs of slacks at $8 each; and two worn pocketbooks at $6 each. All told, you would already have more than a $200 profit. Even when priced at a mere fraction of their original cost, these sales mount up. Remember that Woolworth built his fortune on a nickel-and-dime business.

Pricing Soft Goods

This category includes bed linens, towels, tablecloths, bolts of fabric, curtains and draperies, bedspreads, blankets, and so on—the items that department stores often quaintly refer to as "linens and domestics."

Given a philosophy of low prices for speedy sales, the principal danger here is that your prices might be too low. Soft goods are worth either very little or a great deal. An old linen tablecloth, hand-finished or finished with fine lace, particularly if it was made abroad, can be worth quite a bit of money even if it is many years old. Conversely, a used tablecloth of synthetic fabric probably isn't worth very much since anyone can purchase one from a discount store for very little, with the exact price depending on the size of the cloth. Put yourself in the shoes of a woman, for example, who is browsing through your sale items. Chances are that she didn't come to buy a secondhand tablecloth. She is probably just looking around. Suddenly she spots your tablecloth. "I can use an extra cloth," she thinks. Then she looks at the tag. She might think, "It seems to be in good condition and for a couple of bucks I'll have an extra. Can't lose much—I think I'll take this." However, if the price is on the high side, she might walk away from it, figuring, "She wants $15 for this. I can probably buy a new one for $20 or so. I don't buy a cloth that often—for maybe $5 more I can get a brand-new one and pick the color I prefer."

Of course, as I said, if the cloth is a beautiful *old* one, the price should reflect its unique and special character—you are selling something that has one-of-a-kind heirloom quality. Another cloth of equal vintage and value might not come this way for a long time, if ever. So you have to bounce the arguments back and forth to yourself. The final and best question of all will usually help you decide on the price: What would you be willing to pay for something just like this if you came across it at someone else's sale?

I could go on and on with examples of how to figure prices of individual pieces of merchandise or categories of things. But I've seen literally thousands of items at sales, and it is impossible to suggest actual prices for all the things that all the readers of this book might want to sell. The type of back-and-forth thinking I have suggested will help you come to your own conclusions about individual prices. Have such imaginary conversations with yourself. Put yourself in the shoes of prospective buyers. Ask yourself questions about each of your possessions. You will find that the answers start to spell themselves out, and with increasing rapidity as the game becomes more familiar to you.

7

Creating Advertising That Works

We all know that we can plan and prepare the best party in the world, but if we fail to send out the invitations, no one is going to come. That's how it is with a sale. While it's true that the amount of traffic you will generate may depend on some factors beyond your control, such as the weather, your success depends mostly on other factors over which you have *total* control, such as your advertising and publicity.

People will come out even in rotten weather—and they will come in droves if the sun shines—if you have succeeded in whetting their appetites for some goodies or for some good buys. So give yourself a break: create the best possible advertising copy and the most seductive flyers and signs.

The Serendipity Principle

What you say in your advertisement and how you say it depend on how big or how small a sale you're planning, how much the total merchandise is worth to you, and whether you live in a small town where everyone knows everyone else or a larger suburb or city in which you are acquainted with only a handful of people besides your immediate neighbors.

There is one advertising principle that applies to all situations, to all types of garage sales, without exception. That principle is based on the concept of *serendipity:* the gift of discovering valuable things that are not necessarily being sought. The serendipity principle dictates that your advertisement list or tick off a few specific items you think will be in great demand in your area. People come in the hope of getting one of those advertised items. Then, if the item being sought has already been sold, they comfort themselves by discovering something else they hadn't known they would find.

Let me give you an example. The first time I ever ran a garage sale my husband had just relocated his office and wanted to dispose of a small half-size refrigerator he had used there and no longer needed. I made that the lead item in my newspaper ad. "Half-size refrigerator," I wrote, "suitable for bar, boat, office, basement. Excellent condition, 3 small shelves, holds 4 ice cube trays, door shelves hold beer, soft drinks. Worth much more than the $47 price tag." And it was, too. I probably could have sold this item for $60 to $70 because small refrigerators are hard to find in retail stores, and when new they cost a couple of hundred dollars. But I suspected that the very low price would attract people, that the item would be as interesting to men as to women, and that it would get customers to the sale early. It did all of that.

I confess I felt pretty bad when I had to tell seeker after seeker, "Sorry, it's gone. It went to my very first customer, the moment I opened the sale." One such would-be buyer who had come early, but not early enough, walked out in a huff. Maybe he thought I never even had a half-size refrigerator for sale. But everyone else stayed to browse—after all, they were already there and had nothing to lose—and most of them bought something else. I guess the "inner man," or the "inner woman," likes to feel, "I didn't waste my time. After all, I did find this little whatchamacallit."

Loss Leaders

In another sale, which I ran for a friend, there were hundreds of small items in many categories but no one thing struck me as being a gem that would bring in the treasure hunters. So, on my advice, my friend did something I don't always recommend but which worked well in this instance. I knew that one of my neighbors had an antique brass table lamp that she had talked about selling. She had recently refurbished a room and the lamp no longer suited her decor. I had my friend call her up and ask to buy the lamp. Within minutes the sale was consummated at a fair market price. Then my friend listed this "antique, brass table lamp, mint condition" at a price that was several dollars less than she had paid for it. That item became what is known in retailing as a "loss leader." The small loss was chalked up to the overall expense of running the sale. Because of its fine condition that lamp could have sold twenty times over. Word of its availability brought in many people who might not otherwise have shown up. So try to include in your advertisement some mention of one or more choice items.

Prices in Your Ad

It isn't necessary to list prices for every item you mention in your newspaper advertisement. Some prices can turn off potential customers. For example, sometimes a fine antique piece has to be seen for people to understand what may seem to be a high price. Under such circumstances it could be preferable not to list its price at all. Besides, people like to have some surprises when they browse, and getting them to check the price tag is one way to make them "touch the goods," a selling technique as old as the art of salesmanship.

However, you should definitely mention *some* prices in your ad, particularly if you plan to feature some true bargains. A few prices not only bring in traffic, but they give the reader of the ad a clue as to the type of sale it's going to be. If you list an early American apothecary chest at $495 and an antique French railroad lamp at $350, your reader knows this sale includes more than just rusty old kitchen strainers and nonworking electric percolators. Or, if you were to mention "Complete, matched contents of child's room—bed, dresser, shelves, small rocker, etc., for only $199," a number of people in need of such furniture would show up because they would sense an opportunity to complete an entire room with one purchase at far less than retail prices. So, always mention some prices but not all, picking and choosing carefully those you believe will help, not harm, your sale.

Providing Directions

If your home is in an area that is out of the way or off the beaten path, you will want to give minimum directions on how to find it. You don't need to give every turn and twist of the road, but you might want to say something along this order: "Take Rte. 7 to Dress Barn, turn left up the hill, turn right at Whipaway Drive, follow garage sale signs."

When and Where to Run Your Ads

Let's start with a couple of don'ts. Don't run your advertisement too far in advance of the sale. People forget what does not have a high priority for them. Your sale has a top priority for *you*—after all, you've been planning it and preparing for it for many weeks. But, for casual readers of your local newspaper, the weekend garage sale is low on their list of leisure-time activities—something to do if the advertisement promises special bargains or some sought-after item, or if the location is en route to someplace else they have to go that day.

Ten days to a week before the day you first hang out the "OPEN" sign is the outside limit for placing ads. If you have a local newspaper that comes out daily, run your ad three days, two days, and one day before the sale. Naturally, if your town newspaper is a weekly, you are locked into the day the paper comes out, in which case you will probably do just as well if you run it only the week of the sale and not two or three weeks in a row.

This week-of-the-sale rule does not apply to flyers you may want to distribute or post on local bulletin boards. We will discuss flyer techniques in Chapter 9, but in terms of timing you can put your flyers up two or even three weeks in advance of the sale, provided the owner of the bulletin board doesn't have a limit on how long a flyer or poster can stay in place. If it can remain in place only one week, pick the week of the sale.

How Much to Spend on Advertising

Deciding how much to spend on advertising is as difficult for the garage sale operator as it is for a national advertiser of detergents or beer. There is no absolute way you can determine whether spending another 20 or 30 percent on your ads will generate enough additional business to justify the outlay.

In general, you should spend as much as you need to accomplish your objectives, and not a cent more. This usually means a single piece of copy. Don't run different ads, each with different copy, on different days. You will confuse people and make them think you're a dealer or retailer masquerading as a homemaker with things to sell. That single ad should be the best you are capable of writing, and if you are running it more than once, don't change a word. For one thing, if you keep the copy unchanged, your paper will probably give you a "two times" or "three times" rate, which will be cheaper than running three different blocks of copy on three days.

Your ad is too short if it doesn't have enough lineage to permit you to convince the readers that they really don't want to miss this particular sale. Your ad is too long if it lists every dull and commonplace item you plan to sell, items that people will purchase when they come across them but which are not of sufficient interest to get potential buyers out of the house and into the car.

When you've made a first draft of the copy for your advertisement, ask yourself these questions:

- Have I listed a sufficient *variety* of items to attract people seeking different sorts of merchandise?

- Have I mentioned enough of my low prices so that readers will know *this* sale has some true bargains?

- Have I written the ad in a manner that will state or suggest I have many, many more things than are actually specified in the copy?

- Does the ad sound exciting?

- Have I included the dates of the sale and the hours, as well as directions if the location is difficult to find?

When you're busy with customers, you won't want to be bothered answering the phone to give travel directions. So list your phone number *only* if directions to your home are too complicated to include in the ad.

Perhaps most important of all, ask yourself this question:

If my garage sale ad is one of many similar ads in that issue of the paper, have I included any provocative or enticing statement that will make my sale stand out over others, make mine the one people won't want to miss?

If you look at the samples of sale ads that follow, you'll find copy of this type:

Selling contents of studio apartment—everything priced low for quick sale.

Not just another sale to dispose of basement and attic junk. We've just given up our elegant townhouse and are disposing of entire contents.

A very special sale because it includes more than two dozen early American and English antiques.

My parents have moved to Florida and I'm selling off all their lovely old things for them—many are European treasures and curios.

Our kids have grown up and all of their toys, books, sporting equipment, and den furniture is being sold at very low prices.

We're putting in a new kitchen and are selling all our appliances, kitchenware, cookware, utensils, chairs, etc. Most things in excellent shape and perfect for a second home or weekend retreat.

While it is true that some such explanatory statement as those given above will add to the cost of your advertisement (anywhere from $2 to $10 more, depending on your local classified rates), you should consider this expenditure an investment in your sale. It will more than pay for itself in added traffic.

The ads that follow have been selected from successful advertisements I've written for my own sales and for friends' and clients' sales. They will give you some patterns to follow in creating your own newspaper copy.

GARAGE SALE

Only 50 items, but each a gem. Two matched mahogany chests, Chippendale, $350 pr.; small mahogany drop leaf stand, 2 drawers, $125; 3-

piece set brass fireplace tools, $99; brass student lamp; antique chenille bedspread (double); collection of hardy houseplants; marble cocktail table (best offer over $100); '20s dollhouse; 3-wheel bike; similar one-of-a-kind treasures. Fri.–Sat., 9 a.m. to 4 p.m., 400 Husted Lane, call 724-3516 for directions. No prior sales.

TAG SALE

Selling contents of studio apartment—everything priced low for quick sale. Small walnut desk, 2 drawers ($50); single daybed with very firm mattress ($49); wedge bolsters ($10 pr.); pole lamp, gooseneck lamps, wall lamp; five-drawer pine dresser, very roomy ($45); custom drapes, sill length ($40); full-length closet mirror; set of four dining chairs; bed board for only $5; dishes; glasses; elegant small glass & teak liquor bar; 3 stacking stools; 50 records, mostly classical ($1 each); St. Mary's 100% wool blanket, double; toolchest; electric clocks; bl. and wh. TV set; lots more. Saturday, Aug. 4th, 10 a.m. to 5 p.m. Early Bird Sales: this Friday, 2 p.m. to 6 p.m., Midtown Apartments, 485 Main Street, Apt. 793.

BARN SALE

Everything priced to go in two days. Pine blanket chest, $89; 2 Simmons single pullout beds; 4 lovely Victorian side chairs; 3 tables, antique and reproduction; a very good sofa only $149; stereo; lamps; fireplace equipment; beautiful Louis XV armchair (repro.); b&w TV; 2 matching chairs with needlepoint seats; large, primitive painting, circa 1820, $400 incl. frame; miniature oak desk; wicker porch

furn.; and over 200 small finds from 50¢ to $50.
THIS SAT.-SUN., 10 a.m. to 5 p.m. Deerfield
Rd. corner Newtown Tpke. No prior sales.

GEM-OF-A-TAG SALE

Sat. 11 June, 10 a.m. to 4 p.m., Sun 12 June, 10
a.m. to 2 p.m. Hoover vacuum ($20); floor pol-
isher; Canon 8 mm. movie camera ($25); good
Goodrich tires, F78-14, $20 pr.; professional
beauty parlor hood hair dryer ($40); designer
clothes (some made in Paris), sizes 10 and 12;
Persian lamb sport coat, $35; nearly 100 books;
records; barbecue grill; garden tools; fine brass
candlesticks; antique student lamp (perfect); electric drill ($5); Copymate copier ($20); two W.
African paintings; hot plate; linens; and lots more.
All priced exceedingly low. 247 Kings Highway
(off New Lots).

GARAGE SALE BARGAINS

At our house this coming Friday, Saturday, Sunday, 10 a.m. to 3 p.m. Best item is a mahogany
Governor Winthrop desk, serpentine front, ball
and claw feet, excellent condition, $225. Other
antiques. Also lovely sofa, 84″ long, basically blue,
long, curved back and down cushions. Bicycle,
toys, mower, tractor, tools, and child's chairs and
a blackboard for $5. Pr. stained-glass windows;
weathervane; prints and watercolors; very old rac-
coon coat (suitable either sex), $30; humidifier;
other practical and collectible items too numerous
to list. Old Forest Road between Hickory and
Huckleberry Lanes. Take Rte. 102 to Valeview,
turn right and follow signs.

DOUBLE YARD SALE

Two-home clear-out of furniture, antiques, electric guitar, set of drums, girl's bike, size 9 girl's ice skates, sleds, Royal manual typewriter ($50), AR speakers, KLH radio ($20), old wrought-iron Bible stand ($75), Homelite chainsaw ($59), collection of 50 jigsaw puzzles, Nancy Drew books. Something for everyone. 9 to 5, Fri.–Sat., 23 Green Bay Rd. Park on Clover Leaf Drive.

BRIC-A-BRAC & JUNK SALE

Everything marked at junkyard prices but there are some real gems in the lot. Set of dishes, cookware, flatware, clocks, toaster, garden tools, grill, wallpaper, games, bl. & wh. TV, table lamp, curtains, clothing, crib. Over 350 items. All prices under $99. Friday, 12 to 5; Sat.–Sun. 10 to 4. 690 Deerfield Drive.

STOOP SALE—83 BARROW STREET

Barrow Street has never seen anything like it! For one day only—this Saturday—our stoop and street frontage will become an outdoor "store" featuring furniture and household items from apts. of all 8 tenants in the bldg. PARTIAL LIST: modern daybed in "tweedy" brown ($85); painted white chest, 36″ × 15″ ($99); microscope ($45); infant high chair; fireplace screen; air cond. (12,000 BTU); old oak dressing table; king size headboard (walnut with cane); portable dishwasher ($125); and a fantastic collection of small items (some treasures, some just useful old stuff). Cash & Carry. Park in Municipal lot on Charles Street please. Browsers welcome.

MOVING AWAY SALE

Going west, must sell contents of house immediately. Bedroom, liv. rm., dining rm., patio, including five beds, daybed, sofa. ALSO: Piano ($850), refrig. ($150), Maytag gas dryer ($30), metal shelving units, some antiques, white chest of drawers, white desk, plants, paint, records, laundry equip., contents all kitchen drawers, Fri.–Sat., 10 to 5. Yellow house where Bristol Rd. meets Edgewood Dr.

GARAGE SALE, FURNITURE & MISC.

One day only, Sat. Sept. 12th, 9 to 6. No prior sales. Butcher block dining set, new ($290), Queen Anne leather chair and ottoman, 18th-century antique table, lithographs, paintings, large gold carved-frame mirror ($125), Panasonic color TV, Panasonic reel-to-reel turntable, speakers. Also beer can collection, rare pewter pieces, 20 Wedgwood items, other elegant, choice possessions. 7015 Bayview Drive (betw. Signal Hill & Grove).

GRANDMA'S ATTIC SALE . . . MANY FINE ANTIQUES

Cleaning out Gram's old house before selling it. Round, mahogany, single pedestal, ornately carved parlor table ($250); 2 pine painted corner cupboards ($150 ea.); Sterling demitasse pot (best offer); early European blanket chest with grain painting ($295); 4 yellow Hitchcock chairs, rush seats; oak bureau with carved pulls; antique toys; children's books and nostalgia. Many collectibles incl. stamps, coins, baseball cards. 24 Linden Lane, betw. Moss & Kelmenson. Sat.–Sun. 9 to 3.

YARD SALE

CONDO-BOUND COUPLE SELLING THE PRISTINE CONTENTS OF HOME, BARN, AND WORKSHOP. Heritage Henredon dining table with 3 leaves, pads, 6 chairs. Great collection of wrought-iron pieces including chairs, settee, tables, lounge chairs. Pine bunk beds, small desk, vacuum cleaner, animal travel cage, luggage, dehumidifier, fan, old RCA Victor radio, Weber grill, Sears Kenmore dryer. Complete workshop of small tools. Also: 2 dr. blanket chest, child's chair, dry sink, document boxes. More, lots more, some one-of-a-kind. 185 Redding Ridge Rd. Take Belden Hill to Mt. View, turn left, 2 blocks, turn right, follow signs. Sat.–Sun., 10 to sundown.

8

The Secrets of Good Display

Every retailer knows that *how* you display your merchandise does more than merely tell the customer what you have for sale. The grouping of like items, the catch-all container for inexpensive browsers' bargains, the more elegant treatment of unusual or higher-priced items—all of these things carry unspoken messages.

There are some fundamental retail techniques and practices that also apply to garage sales. Here they are.

Plotting Your Selling Area

It is true that people like surprises when they go to garage sales and that some degree of jumble in a small area can work in your favor. But people also like to stroll around. They like the carnival or flea market atmosphere. By spreading out some of your items, you convey the impression that you have sufficient merchandise to have justified the customer's trip, and you make it possible for a buyer to take a leisurely, pleasant stroll around the various displays of goods. So plan to use your garage, your driveway, your terrace, or even the road-front space or sidewalk in front of your house if local regulations permit and if you have someone to man the area. Include whatever outdoor and indoor space is available, *but not the inside of your home unless all the furniture in the house is for sale,* in which case it is to your advantage to show things in their proper setting. More on this below.

Creating Counter Space

You are going to need as many counter areas as you can possibly devise. Card tables make excellent display surfaces. A door or a couple of wooden boards placed across two sawhorses provide sturdy surfaces on which to arrange sale items. (You can probably borrow extra sawhorses from your neighbors.) A wheelbarrow or two to hold small, unrelated items that will not be injured if carelessly tossed around can be dressed up with crepe paper or ribbon on the handles. If you do use such wheelbarrows, be sure to put a tag on each with the inscription "THIS WHEELBARROW IS *NOT* FOR SALE." Otherwise, you will surely have several disappointed would-be buyers.

An outdoor picnic table can also function as a counter that will hold heavy items—and quite a few of them at that. The matching picnic benches give you still more space. Even your kitchen table, moved into the garage and covered with a cloth to avoid scratching, could be a display counter.

Be certain that every table is sturdy enough to withstand a certain amount of careless jostling. Strangers are sometimes less careful of the props than you, the proprietor, might be. If one of your tables seems a bit rickety but you still need to use it, place it up against a wall for extra support. It's a good idea to put only soft goods (linens, etc.) on such a table so that, should it topple, no merchandise will be broken or damaged.

Draping Your Counter Space

Except for picnic tables, it's a good idea to use cloths or colored sheets to cover each piece of furniture on which you plan to place your goods. They lend a more professional and colorful tone to your temporary store and, if such covers are selected with care, they can also serve to highlight some types of merchandise to their best advantage.

Something like a redwood picnic table is not likely to suffer scuff marks, so it need not be covered. But most other surfaces should be draped. This will prevent scratching of good tables and will make planks and doors used across sawhorses look less makeshift. (If everything about your sale looks junky, you will have to settle for junk prices.)

You probably have in your home a number of things that you can use as covers: tablecloths, colored or patterned sheets that can easily be tossed into the washing machine after the sale, yard goods left over from your last sewing project, lightweight bedspreads (avoid white) such as those Indian madras ones so popular as throws in college dormitories, or any length of fabric picked up at the remnant counter of a fabric store. If you're not too particular about color, you'll find plenty of odds and ends on the store's remnant table and they won't cost very much. Whatever costs you do incur can be chalked up to the budget you will be allowing for the entire sale. Some of it can even be recouped if, during the last hours of the event, when most merchandise is gone, you pin to each fabric remnant a visible sign saying, "THIS PIECE OF FABRIC, XX¢," setting some low price such as 99¢, depending on what you paid for it and its serviceability.

Making Your Higher-Priced Items Look Valuable

Did you ever notice that when you go to a jeweler and ask to be shown a precious piece of jewelry—perhaps a diamond or an expensive gold bracelet—the shopkeeper won't just lay it on the counter or hand it to you? He will first ceremoniously whip out a black velvet pad or cloth and then lay the precious item on it. This tells you something. It says: "What we have here is so valuable I don't want to mar or scratch it by laying it on any old surface." Then, when you hear the high price, you're not so surprised. You've been tipped off that this is "special goods."

I've had excellent results from displaying rare or important pieces on a special counter covered with a black cloth. Black velvet, if you can find an inexpensive remnant, is the best; but inexpensive, shiny, black lining material, neatly trimmed and draped over a table, also does a fine job of indicating to the public that this particular display holds higher-priced items to be handled with care. A small standing display sign that states: "VALUABLE ITEMS. PLEASE HANDLE WITH CARE" goes a step further in making your statement.

In one of my garage sales I wanted to dispose of a glass *objet d'art* made by Baccarat. My husband and I had received it as a wedding present many years before and neither of us ever liked it. In fact, we were never certain whether it had any utilitarian purpose or whether it was just a work of art to be gazed at with pleasure. A friend once said, "What a charming nut dish!" and someone else suggested I use it to float a single gardenia in a bit of water. Well, it didn't give us any special pleasure and we decided to sell it.

I had no knowledge of its value but suspected that our little piece of glass was worth quite a bit. On a trip to New York I stopped into Baccarat and showed them my glass doodad. I was told they no longer made that particular item but that in the year that it was given to me it had cost $85. Since then, I was informed, prices of Baccarat objects had increased considerably and what with inflation, had this particular item still been in the line, it would have cost approximately $200.

Well, I knew no one was going to give me $200 for this shiny bit of glass unless some Baccarat collector chanced along, and the likelihood of that happening was zero. I decided to sell it for the $85 it had cost originally and, even at that, it would take a person knowledgeable about Baccarat to appreciate its value. I took a cardboard box from my attic, stapled black velvet around the sides and the closed end, and thus created a raised platform on which I would later place the glass object. With a few whacks of my staple gun, I mounted a white cardboard placard to the back of the box. I lettered this legend: "BACCARAT objet d'art. Rare collector's find. Appraised by Baccarat at $200. OUR PRICE: $85." It sold to a very pleased man who said that while he did not collect Baccarat in particular, he considered this an investment that would grow in value.

The Legend That Sells

Generally speaking, I have found that legends or descriptive information about items that do not speak for themselves help stimulate interest in pieces that might otherwise be overlooked or undervalued. I ran a garage sale for a woman who had, for many years before they became popular in this country, collected French *affiches*, those art gallery posters that can now be found in some department stores and in many art galleries. Her collection went back more than twenty years and she had posters announcing Paris exhibits that had taken place in the 1950s and '60s. She wanted to sell them all because she was moving to a small apartment. I carefully tacked ten of these posters to one wall inside her garage and placed small price tickets alongside each. In the center of the display I hung a long, vertical cardboard with this legend: "FRENCH ART EXHIBIT POSTERS (AFFICHES). One of a kind. Many old and rare. Priced from $2 to $20. You'd pay much more for them in an art store. Ask to see others." The interest in this art display was tremendous and my client sold all of the fifty posters she had, including those on the garage wall. One woman bought eight to send to her daughter who was away at college and needed something colorful with which to decorate her room.

I would also suggest legends on price tags, where they are called for and when the tag is of a sufficient size to carry your story. For instance, if you have a riding lawnmower for sale, you might do more than just put a price on the tag. Type your information on a paper sticker and affix it to one side of the tag with the price on the other side. The copy might read like this: "This International Harvester Riding Mower is in perfect working condition. Just had its annual servicing (including cleaning, new spark plugs, oil change) at I.H. dealership on Deerfield Ave., which will pick up and deliver I.H. mowers. This machine can be operated by man, woman, or teenager—very easy, makes mowing fun. Will demonstrate."

Of course, most of the items in your garage sale won't need any explanation. A barbecue grill is a barbecue grill, a rake is a rake, and an iron skillet is an iron skillet. It is only when something about the item is not self-evident, or when a special selling point needs to be made, or when the merchandise is valuable, that you will want to offer information. Limit your legends to those special cases.

Were you to hype every piece of unimportant merchandise, you might give the impression that you were trying too hard to dispose of things. Most of the goods will speak for themselves. Let them. Underselling often serves you better than overselling—except in instances such as I have described.

Displaying Clothes

If you have used clothing for sale, and if the number of garments is great enough to justify it, you will want to rent a clothing rack on which to display this merchandise. Some people actually purchase such a rack for their sale because it's something they have wanted to own for a long time but never got around to buying. Anyone who doesn't have enough closet space to store winter clothes in summer and vice versa should consider buying a rack as a permanent household possession. An attic or dry basement or a laundry room or playroom is where most people store them, and racks can usually be dismantled and kept in a very small space when not in use.

Whether you buy, rent, or borrow such a rack, you will find it of enormous help in displaying clothing at your sale. It's a lot easier for a browser to examine garments that are hanging. It makes the clothing look better, too. However, I have also had very good results from a display of men's suits and sweaters laid out on a clean, dry lawn. If you follow this approach, be certain that there is sufficient space (aisles) between the rows of garments so that shoppers can walk around without stepping on the merchandise and that there is no dew on the ground to leave spots on the garments.

Some of your used clothing might call for a bit of explanation and, here again, your labels or tags can be used to carry such legend copy: "Note the Bergdorf-Goodman label." "Lining is hand-finished." "Double-breasted suits are back in style." "Worn less than half a dozen times . . . I gained weight." "Fake furs like this are kicky for college kids." "Portuguese fisherman's sweater." "Remember how cold it was last winter? This year may be even worse and this coat is *very* warm!" "No reasonable price refused. Name *yours*."

The Try-on Area

Most people who buy secondhand clothing want an opportunity to try on the garments since they can't be returned if they don't fit. This means you're going to need a small area set aside for trying on clothes, along with a mirror, preferably one that is full-length. It isn't advisable to permit people into your home, which is going to be off limits if you follow the advice in Chapter 13, unless the person is someone you know or unless you're prepared to leave the sale area and go inside with your prospective customer.

An ideal arrangement is to hang a sheet or cloth in one corner of your garage and place a mirror behind it. Then your customers can try on garments without being conspicuous. However, on those occasions when I have run a sale and lacked sufficient space to spare inside the garage, I've set the mirror against the side of the house or garage, picking the side where no displays have been set up. By making it possible for customers to try on garments away from the center of the sale area you achieve a semiprivate feeling. You will also find that many people are satisfied just to slip things on over their own clothes. While a special try-on area can sometimes be eliminated, the availability of a mirror is a must.

In general, you should adopt these basic display principles:

- Make your merchandise easy to see and easy to reach.

- Make items as clean and attractive as possible.

- Allow the maximum walk-around space so that things don't get knocked about and tables aren't pushed out of place.

- Have some surprises.

- If you sell clothing, make it possible for people to examine the items and try them on.

- Give expensive items a luxury display of their own.

- Let your tags act as silent salesmen by writing appropriate legend copy on them.

9

Flyers, Posters, and Signs

In addition to your newspaper advertisement, you will want to create other promotional tools that will help publicize your garage sale in as many ways, to as many people, as is economically feasible.

The first thing you're going to need is what professional direct mail people call a flyer. A flyer can be defined as a printed piece that gives information about a sale or any other activity you are promoting—anything from a local concert to the opening of a car wash emporium. Flyers are either mailed or delivered to people who might be potential buyers of the goods or service being sold.

In direct mail a flyer can take the form of a very expensive, multicolored, printed and folded piece that tells the reader a great deal about the item or items for sale. In the case of your garage sale, however, you can do with a much simpler and quite inexpensive piece. In fact, you can make it yourself and the only costs you are likely to incur will be those of the paper and printing. Should you have free access to a copying machine, the flyer will cost you no more than the price of the paper.

The sort of flyer you will want will work nicely on an ordinary 8½-by-11-inch sheet of paper. I prefer colored stock—yellow or light green for high visibility of the type, but any color that will stand out on a bulletin board will do. If you can't buy a ream of these colored sheets inexpensively in your local stationery store, settle for ordinary white typing paper. It will serve your purpose. Color does catch the eye more quickly, however, when a flyer is competing for attention with many other notices on a display board. I happen to think it's worth the small difference in cost.

The flyer you create is going to be used in three ways. You're going to post it on bulletin boards in your community where people are likely to see it. You're going to leave small stacks of them with friendly area merchants and antique dealers who don't mind having them on the checkout counter or elsewhere in the shop. And you're going to distribute some of them to homes in your neighborhood.

Posting and Distributing Your Flyer

I have found that local laundromats are good places to leave these flyers—they don't compete for counter space with merchandise the proprietor is trying to sell. I have also found that any antique shop owner I know or to whom I give advance notice of my garage sale (usually through a personal visit to his or her store, at which time I have a supply of flyers under my arm) is willing to set out a stack where customers and browsers can pick them up. If you are personally acquainted with any store owner—and the type of store doesn't matter—don't fail to request permission to leave some flyers there. A friend will rarely turn you down.

In the chapter on apartment house tag sales I will describe how I use these flyers to great advantage by distributing them to residents of the apartment building where the sale is to take place. Similarly, you can have one of the youngsters in your family, a high school teenager, or the boy who delivers the local paper house to house, distribute these flyers to people in your neighborhood.

It is illegal to put anything in a mailbox other than mail that has gone through the post office, but some people get around this regulation by taping flyers to the outside of area mailboxes, or by rolling them up and shoving them under the little handle that opens the box. As long as you don't put anything *inside* the box, it's legal.

Putting your flyers under the windshields of cars in the parking lot of your nearby shopping center is yet another way to inform individuals of your sale. The disadvantage of this technique is that some people will throw the flyer on the ground and you should really be prepared to send someone around at the end of the day to pick up the papers that have been discarded in this manner.

What to Put on Your Flyer

While the small size of your newspaper advertisement limits the number of sale items you can mention, and requires that you speak in a form of shorthand, your flyer offers you an excellent opportunity to expand on your message.

The simplest type of flyer is a typewritten sheet with a printed headline that says "GARAGE SALE" (or whatever yours is called). You can decorate it with the outline of a giant tag and put your copy inside the illustration. If it's a barn sale, you might type your copy inside a simple drawing of a barn. And so on. If you have artistic talent, draw on it to create an attention-getting illustration of your own design.

One caution: be sure that your illustration is not art for the sake of art alone. Be certain of these factors:

- The artwork must serve to telegraph a message about the nature of your happening.

- The illustration must not take so much space that

you shortchange yourself in the area left for promotional copy.

- Understanding your illustration should not be dependent on the use of different colors because, when you reproduce your flyer, the copies will be black on white or black on colored paper.

After the caption or headline, you should provide a few sentences that promote your particular event. Keep in mind that during certain seasons of the year you may be competing for customers with other people running similar sales in your area. So a brief paragraph of copy that sets your sale apart from the rest is in order. Whatever theme you used in your newspaper ad is what you should pick up here. For example, if you wrote in your ad, "Disposing contents of our second home" or "Ceiling-to-basement clearance of first-rate home furnishings" or "We're moving and don't plan to take any of our home furnishings with us . . . everything goes in this sale . . . at ridiculously low prices," then that's the copy you will use in your lead paragraph.

Use the rest of the page to list and describe as many of your best items as you can fit onto the sheet. The more things you mention, the more people will be attracted. On the next few pages of this chapter, you will find some examples of how the copy for your flyer might be handled.

Getting It Written

Here's a suggestion on how to get your flyer copy written without sweat. Think of the major items or categories of items in your sale. Then write the copy pertinent to each of those items or categories on an individual three-by-five-inch card. When you have all the cards prepared, shuffle them around on your desk until you have created a sequence or mix that seems reasonable to you. Next, estimate whether all the copy you have put on the cards will fit on your flyer page.

IT'S A GEM-OF-A-TAG-SALE! Sat. 11 June, 10 a m. to 4 p.m., Sun 12 June, 10 a m. to 2 p m. Hoover Vacuum ($20); floor polisher; Canon 8mm movie camera ($30); good Goodrich tires, F78-14 ($10 pr.); professional beauty parlor hair dryer ($40); designer clothes (Paris suit, Bergdorf, Saks, etc.), sizes 10 & 12; Persian lamb sport coat ($25) (remember last winter's freeze? . . . you can line a raincoat with it); nearly 100 books, records; barbecue grill; iron; garden tools; fine brass candlesticks; antique student lamp (mint condition); objets d'art; electric drill ($5); Copymate copier; two W. African paintings; hot plate; linens; French art gallery posters; and lots more, all priced exceedingly low.

247 Kings Highway
(off New Lots)

ALSO: Antique radio; guitar; old iron floor lamp

SELLING CONTENTS OF STUDIO APARTMENT—EVERYTHING
PRICED LOW FOR QUICK SALE

Small walnut desk, 2 drawers ($50), single daybed with very firm
Stearns & Foster mattress ($49), wedge bolsters ($10 pr), pole
lamp, gooseneck lamps, wall lamp, 5-drawer pine dresser, very
roomy ($45), contemporary sofa ($99), Lord & Taylor custom
drapes, sill length ($30), full-length closet mirror, also round
foyer mirror, set of 4 dining chairs, bed board for only $5, dishes,
glasses, elegant small glass & teak liquor bar, 3 stacking stools;
9' × 12' wool rug ($95 with underpad), kitchen utensils, 50 rec-
ords, mostly classical ($1 each), St Mary's 100% wool blanket,
double size, bed pillows, tool chest, kitchen shelves (4 shelves,
$5), electric clocks, black & white TV set, TV stand, and lots
more

SATURDAY, AUGUST 4th, 10 a m to 4 p m
EARLY BIRD SALES this Friday, 2 p m to 6 p m

MADISON TOWERS—APT 15L

All sales cash-and-carry—no deliveries

YARD SALE

COME!
BROWSE!
ENJOY!

MAY 14-15

This is not just another run-of-the-mill attic clearance We are moving to a sunbelt condo and are disposing of the entire contents of our 9-room house

THE DATE: Saturday & Sunday
May 14-15
THE HOURS: 10 to dusk on Saturday
10 to 4 on Sunday

THE ADDRESS:
150 Wilson Avenue
(between Signal Hill Rd
and Grover Ave)

HERE ARE JUST A HANDFUL OF THE ITEMS IN OUR SALE

WALNUT WALL UNIT SHELVES
Eight lovely shelves, not a scratch on them. Includes a 16" shelf for records.
OUR PRICE: $140

MODERN DAYBED
Wooden frame (teak) and fabric is brown/orange plaid When the back cushions are removed, the extrafirm cushion-seat makes a fine guest accommodation.
OUR PRICE: $85

OAK DRESSER ...
... with swinging mirror. A rare antique find these days. Has marble slab cut to fit top
OUR PRICE: $220

RECLINER
Soft, brown vinyl, washes clean with damp sponge Great for TV watching or doing T.M
OUR PRICE: $79

CRYSTAL GOBLETS
Set of 8 crystal goblets with matching wine glasses. All silver rimmed. Worth much more than our Yard Sale price.
OUR PRICE: $88

DESK & CHAIR
Handsome desk, teak, brass knobs on one large, three small, and one center drawer Matching coffee-colored swivel desk chair with chrome base.
OUR PRICE: $199

PLUS. Two typewriters, Christmas ornaments, Singer console sewing machine, easel, golf cart, two fake Tiffany lamps, and much, much more

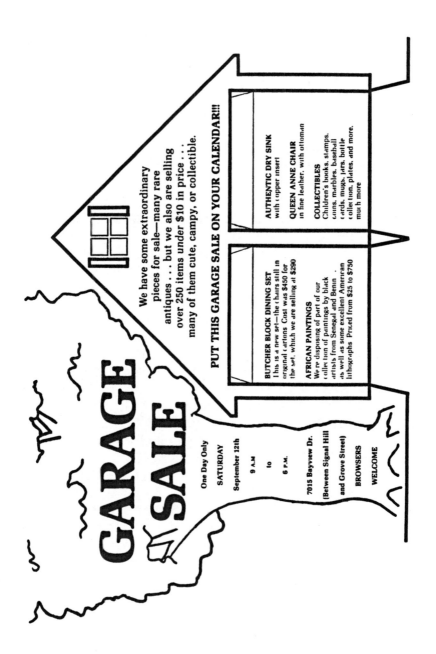

If you think you have too much, eliminate those cards that seem expendable. Finally, copy the cards you've retained onto a sheet of paper. If it runs too long, delete every word that seems superfluous. Conversely, if you don't seem to have very much copy for the sheet, prowl your house, take another look at the merchandise you have accumulated for the event and see if you haven't overlooked some attractive piece or some group of miscellaneous items that would enable you to write something along these lines: "Over fifty odds and ends from our kitchen and bar" or "Close to fifty pieces of children's clothing and toys" or "Over a hundred odds and ends, most in excellent condition, including dishes, pots, linens, electrical supplies, garden equipment, and much more."

Then, of course, your flyer should give the address, the date and hours of the sale, the rain date, if any, and instructions for locating the sale site, which you can spell out in greater detail in your flyer than in your ad.

If you believe that your sale is extraordinary or unusual in any way, don't hesitate to make that point in your flyer. Just above the address, as a closing to your sell copy, you might say, "OUR FIRST TAG SALE AND IT'S GOING TO BE AN EXTRAORDINARY ONE . . . a lifetime's possessions covering a broad range of merchandise." Or, "NOT JUST ANOTHER NEIGHBORHOOD JUNK SALE . . . we're including some of our finest antiques and lovely furniture." Or maybe, "YOU WON'T FIND PRECIOUS ANTIQUES OR HEIRLOOMS AT THIS SALE . . . IT'S STRICTLY A JUNK SALE . . . BUT WHAT EXTRAORDINARY JUNK! AND WHAT LOW PRICES! Remember what that famous philosopher, *Unknown,* said: 'One woman's junk is another's treasure!' So don't miss our sale. WE EXPECT IT WILL BE LOTS OF JUNKY FUN FOR EVERYONE."

Flyers vs. Posters

When your flyer goes up on a bulletin board it becomes a poster. However, the word *poster* usually implies a large-sized announcement of some event or activity. It employs a minimum of words, which is what differentiates it from a flyer. The latter can go into considerable detail while poster copy is kept brief to convey a quick message to someone who is moving past it rather quickly. In the advertising business, the billboards you see from your car are known as posters. Next time you look at one, notice how brief and telegraphic the message is.

Now, it is possible that, in addition to your flyer, you might want to create such a poster, which can be as large as the space available for hanging it. Aim to create one that is colorful, decorative, and tells merely the name of the event (garage sale), the dates, hours, the place, and perhaps a single line of sell copy ("MORE THAN 500 ITEMS"; "THE GARAGE SALE TO END THEM ALL"; "BROWSERS WELCOME"; "DO YOUR CHRISTMAS SHOPPING EARLY"; "RECORDS, Records, records . . . BOOKS, Books, books . . . CLOTHES, Clothes, clothes!")

Unless you have a specific spot in mind for your poster and know that there will be room for it, you may find it more difficult to post than a flyer. If you have a choice between a flyer and a poster, take the former—its long copy provides more opportunity to whet the appetite of prospective customers. On the other hand, if someone in your family or a friend owns a local store and is willing to put one of your posters into the store window, grab the opportunity. While people won't usually stop at a store window long enough to read a lot of detailed copy on a flyer, they will notice a large poster and get the message quickly if the words are kept to a minimum.

Posting Your Flyers

For most people, the flyer does double duty: it serves as a poster on bulletin boards and as a handout. There are lots of places where flyers can be tacked up. Many local stores, including your neighborhood supermarkets, laundromats, discount stores, and sometimes five-and-ten chain stores, as well as bookstores, bakeries, and beauty parlors, have bulletin boards where you can post a flyer free of charge. Don't limit yourself to the supermarket where you happen to do your own shopping. If there are others in your area, use their bulletin boards as well.

When you go out to post your flyers, be sure to take some thumbtacks with you. Don't count on finding some unused ones on the board—there is a fifty-fifty chance you won't find any. If the boards on which you are posting your message are not too crowded, the best place to put your notice is at the center of the panel at approximate eye level for someone about 5'6" tall. If you find that an entire bulletin board is taken up with other notices, look through them and see if some have expired; that is, if there is notice of a meeting or event that has already taken place. Many people fail to come by and remove their signs after their happening has become history. It is considered proper—in fact, you will be doing everyone a favor—if you remove outdated notices and place them in a trash can. Doing so will make room for your own announcement.

You're going to be surprised at how many people read the stuff on these bulletin boards. Your readers will include mothers looking for available baby-sitters (and often children's clothes, toys, and furniture); young people interested in apartments for rent (and perhaps secondhand furniture and kitchen equipment as well); people who are curious about local plays, concerts, movies, etc., who will also be the people who have enough leisure time to browse at garage sales; people who just moved to town and are interested in knowing what's going on, and who often need a thousand-and-one things for the house. So don't be surprised when you ask the customers at your sale, "Did you see our ad in the paper?" and they reply, "No. I believe I read about it on a bulletin board."

Creating Your Road Signs

A road sign has even less copy on it than a poster, and its

principal functions are to tell passersby that there's a sale in the neighborhood and to direct people to the premises. Except for apartment house sales, we can assume that all but the neighbors within walking distance will arrive at your home by automobile.

Many people running their first garage sale forget that what you can read on a sign that's on your desk is quite different from what you can read from your moving automobile when the sign is on a roadside pole. The first rule is this: if it isn't legible or understandable from a vehicle that is twenty-five to thirty feet away, it isn't going to do you much good.

That doesn't mean that every word needs to be legible from that distance. Signs speak in shorthand. An arrow pointing in the direction of the road to be taken or a picture of a large tag with the word "TODAY" printed on it delivers your message. What you must avoid are words on the sign that are so small a person would have to get out of the car and walk to the sign in order to know what it says. No one is going to do that.

Consider using road signs that are merely large cutout arrows with the word "SALE" on them or a large cutout tag with an arrow or the address. Or try a piece of ordinary cardboard with an arrow, a date, an address, or whatever is most necessary for your particular event. One current vogue is to use paper plates as signs, but I find them too small for the message unless they are being used for every other sign, alternating with others that are large enough to carry the word. I really don't understand why people use paper plates except that they happen to be around the house. To me a paper plate says, "Come to our picnic." It doesn't communicate the nature of the event.

You should place your signs at all those intersections where someone could make a wrong turn if he or she didn't know the neighborhood very well. And, as you get closer to your home, signs should be spaced shorter distances apart. Very close to your driveway, you might have a sign reading,

"SLOW DOWN . . . SALE AHEAD." If you have special parking instructions—"Park on gravel"; "Park in driveway"; "DO NOT BLOCK DRIVEWAY, *please!*; or "Park both sides"—these should be posted within walking distance of the sale site.

If you don't want anyone to park in your driveway, either because you plan to use that area for merchandise displays or because your driveway isn't wide enough for a departing vehicle to pass one that's arriving, you can successfully block the head of your driveway by placing your own car there. The bumper or back of your car then affords you a nice display surface for a large sign reading, "WELCOME TO OUR GARAGE SALE. Please park on road."

Marking the Site of the Sale

If you don't use the back of your car as a display area, you will nonetheless want to have some large sign out front that says, "GARAGE SALE TODAY" or "SALE . . . HERE."

Another device I use serves a dual purpose. It identifies the premises of the sale and prevents people from parking on a soft grassy area where tire marks may be difficult to eradicate. I get a dozen stakes (the kind of poles I use in my tomato garden) and insert them in the ground, equal distances apart. Then I run a strong piece of string from pole to pole, wrapping the string tightly around each pole so that it doesn't slip down.

I then tear up an old colored sheet for which I no longer have any use and make pennants out of the pieces. By folding the broad end of the pennant over the string and stapling it in place, I get a wonderful and colorful effect. Should you employ this technique, and if there should happen to be a bit of a breeze, you will have an attractive, attention-getting device that tells passersby that something very special is going on at your house.

Another gimmick that attracts customers is to park your family's cars, and perhaps one of your neighbor's as well, along the road near your house. This gets the cars out of your garage area and, at the same time, helps create the impression that something of a party nature is going on beyond the driveway. There is an old retail saying that "everyone likes to shop on a busy street." The maxim certainly holds true for garage sales.

Unless the forecast is for rain the day your sale is to open, it is better to put up the signs the evening before the curtain is scheduled to go up, but allow enough lead time so you can finish before darkness sets in. You're going to have quite a bit to do on morning number one and this is one activity that can be done in advance. Of course, if the signs go up *before* sale time, you want to be sure they mention the days of the event. Otherwise you're going to have some people driving in before you're ready for them. Customers are what you are looking for, but not twelve hours ahead of schedule.

Color Me Legible

The crayon or paint you use in making your road signs should be a dark color. Yellow doesn't read well from a distance, nor does light green or any soft pastel, though these are excellent colors for the cardboard stock you might use. Black, navy, and dark brown are good for communicating at a distance. If you want to add a colorful touch to the sign, use the bright colors—red. orange, brilliant blue, or bright green—as decorative touches.

The making of flyers, posters, and signs may take a bit more thought and time than you anticipate. Be sure you allow sufficient time before the sale weekend so that you don't have to toss off these important promotional devices in a burst of frenzy. Allow adequate time so that you can make additional signs if you find you have shortchanged yourself. And be sure to allow enough time for posting signs. You may need as much as an hour or even more to circle your neighborhood and locate the turns and intersections where signs seem necessary.

An Important Caution

Be certain that you inquire of your local police department or planning and zoning board regarding any rules that might be in effect in your town concerning the posting of signs. Many towns have no such rules or regulations. But with the increase in recent years in the number of sales run in some areas, many local governments have established rules about where you may or may not post signs.

Telephone poles are private property belonging to the phone company and posting on them is usually forbidden. Tacking signs to trees is sometimes illegal if the trees are on private property. You would be well advised to ask the property owner before you hang something on one of his or her trees. I have never had a property owner turn me down if I asked nicely and promised to remove the sign after the event. However, taking someone's generosity for granted can sometimes lead to having your signs removed and discarded. So be nice. Ask! And, of course, be certain that you remove *all* your signs when you have rung down the curtain on your money-maker.

10

Promotional Ideas, Secrets, and Tricks That Move Lots of Odds and Ends

Having grown up in the age of retailing, you've been exposed to cut-price sales, two-for-one sales, money-back guarantees, cents-off coupons, going-out-of-business sales, fire sales, cash rebates, and a host of other marketing techniques designed to make you buy *now*. All of these techniques work—on some people, with some merchandise. And most of them are honest and legitimate selling tools.

The reasons those sales approaches continue to be popular with the average honest retailer is that they *do* work. They bring in the customers and promote what the trade calls impulse buying. Even when they don't create a sale, they do a good job of creating an image for the store: this place is run by a lively go-getter who wants to give you a good deal when you buy here.

Some of these retailing techniques work equally well at garage sales. Here are some merchandising devices or techniques (you might even call them gimmicks, the name doesn't matter) that never fail.

Two-for-One Book Special

One of the items in your home most difficult to dispose of is old books. All of us have books on our shelves that no one in the family is ever going to read again or use for reference. While some books live forever, there are many that we all manage to accumulate that are only of passing interest. But books are things that most people can't even give away. Local hospitals will usually accept only classics or currently popular books. The best-sellers of five years ago aren't very popular with patients and the book cart lady doesn't want to drag around a lot of heavy stuff no one wants to read.

You will also find that your local charity stores or resale establishments are often reluctant to take your old books, as is your local library. There are, of course, exceptions to this. If you want to donate a first edition of a rare and out-of-print book, you will find many takers. Or if you want to dispose of books that are still on the best-seller list, your library will probably be happy to take them off your hands. Generally speaking, however, unimportant books stay around the house long after they are of interest to you, merely because no one is willing to accept them.

You can, however, sell many, if not all, of these books by keeping the prices ridiculously low—anything from 25¢ to $2, depending on how recently the book was popular and who the author is. Putting up a sign on the book table that says, "Buy one . . . and another marked with the same price is yours F-R-E-E" creates an irresistible bargain. Nowadays, with paperbacks selling for as much as $4 or even $5, anything between hard covers that's priced at 99¢ is considered dirt cheap. *Two* for 99¢ is too good to pass up. And paperbacks at 25¢ or 50¢, with a second one tossed in free, will also race off the premises. So if your aim is to get rid of several dozen books, "Buy One . . . Get One Free" is the sure way to accomplish that and make some dough in the bargain.

Discounts for Senior Citizens

A pleasant touch that won't end up costing too much of

your proceeds is to offer 15 percent off to senior citizens. You can, of course, limit the discount to special merchandise only—things you have in quantity, such as books or records or clothing, or odds and ends that are not likely to be fought over by customers. In my garage sales I also offer 15 percent off on records and books to students. You will be amazed, if you use this gimmick, at how many of your customers are suddenly going to school! You might prefer to limit such discounts to 10 percent or, on a few categories of items, raise it as high as 20 percent. You're not going to believe this, but I have overheard whispered conversations between two browsers and watched surreptitious exchanges of money that convinced me someone who didn't fit the "senior" or "student" category was arranging for a friend or offspring to handle the transaction in order to get this saving—and sometimes the saving is no more than 15¢ or 25¢. I smile and close my eyes to those undercover arrangements and I don't ask for proof that someone is a student or senior. After all, the purpose of your sale is to move out a lot of stuff you don't want, and if this does it, all to the good. If the discounted price is going to be less than that for which you want to sell an item, you should put a higher price on it. For some customers the whole thing becomes a game—the object being to get what they want for as little as possible. You're going to be amazed at how many people ask for the discount or ask you to discount a particular item that is not included in your special discount group. Discounts do, indeed, clinch many a sale.

The Jumble Box

When planning your sale and sorting out stuff to be sold, you will find that your kitchen drawers and cabinets and your linen closet, as well as your garage, basement, attic, and toolshed, yield a large number of small, low-value items. Most of them will be things you would ordinarily come across by accident and, realizing that you no longer use

them, would throw in the rubbish can. Hold it! Add up the
nickels and dimes and quarters and dollars that all these
items might produce and you have another $10 or $20,
perhaps more—enough to pay for your advertising and even
your tags and stickers. So don't throw anything away. One
of the sharpest antique dealers in New England once told
me, "There's a customer for everything. Just be patient and
someone will surely come along who will buy it."

The best way to attract attention to these low-ticket items
is to put them into a jumble box or barrel or bin of some
sort. An ordinary cardboard box, about the size that your
supermarket gets its oranges and apples shipped in (or two
such boxes if you have enough merchandise) is perfectly
adequate for this type of container. If you want to make it
look good, you can fancy it up by putting plain brown
wrapping paper or inexpensive gift wrapping paper from
your rewrap box around the sides. Then just load items into
this dump display. Be sure the items you include are unbreakable as they will be subjected to a lot of handling.

Affix a sign to the box on which you have lettered something like this: "Every Item in This Box under 99¢." Or,
"Take Any Item in This Box for Only 50¢." Or, "EXPLORE
THIS BOX. NOTHING OVER $2." An ordinary laundry
shirt cardboard is good enough for this sign.

If you have some larger items that don't fit into the
carton, place them on the ground, very close to the jumble
box. A wheelbarrow makes an excellent dump display, too,
for similarly inexpensive and unbreakable items.

One caution: sometimes a browser will pick an item off a
table, carry it around for a bit, then—deciding not to buy it
after all—drop it into one of your bargain containers. These
customers don't mean to hurt your sale in any way. It just
happens to be the nearest container at the moment they
decide against buying the item. So you have to check these
containers once in a while during the sale hours. It can be
embarrassing if someone picks an expensive piece of merchandise out of the jumble box and tells you, "Well, the sign

says it should be under $2." Most customers, when told someone had inadvertently dropped it into the wrong container, will accept the explanation without fuss. Once in a while, however, you will get a disbeliever. So keep your eyes peeled for this sort of thing.

Useless, Worthless, and Broken Items

Sometimes a very candid admission of an article's worthlessness creates a sale. Some people, when told up front that something doesn't work or is broken, will see this as a challenge to their ingenuity in fixing things or as an opportunity to get a terrific bargain by buying something cheap and then finding an unexpected or novel use for the item.

I always have one table or display spot on which I feature, by way of a sign, "USELESS, WORTHLESS, AND BROKEN ITEMS AT USELESS, WORTHLESS, AND BROKEN PRICES." A nonworking old electric iron makes a good doorstop for someone. A nonfunctioning electric percolator, shown with a couple of flowers in it, suggests an innovative vase. In the last chapter of this book you'll read the story of two garage sale customers who got into a serious fight over a broken hibachi I had for sale. One was a plumber who felt he could use his welding equipment to repair the hibachi and the other was a woman who wanted to use it as a planter on her terrace. I have sold nonworking cameras, broken old watches, even my old reading glasses. Pots without lids, cast-off doorknobs, antiquated toasters, rusty scissors, faded kerchiefs, even a rickety ironing board that shook like it had palsy—I have sold them all, making room for new and better-functioning items.

Just don't try to kid someone that something can be "easily fixed" or "just needs a minor repair." People resent that sort of thing if the statement lacks credibility. On the other hand, telling them that something really isn't very good, or that you haven't been able to make it work, will often present a challenge they can't resist.

Museum Quality

Another interesting approach is to make a *plus* out of an item's extreme old age. With antiques hard to find and growing daily in value, many people who have space in their homes like to hang on to very old items in the belief that, with time, they will grow more valuable. There is truth in this belief and, if people had enough space to hoard everything they own but no longer use, there would probably be no garage sales. But most of us have closets that look like the ones that old radio character, Fibber McGee, used to have—when you open the door, the contents fall out. The overstuffed closet is really at the root of all garage sales. People simply don't have enough closet space for the possessions they have managed to accumulate over a lifetime of acquisition.

If you do have some truly old or outdated possessions that cannot properly be classified as antiques, the legends on such items can *suggest* that, in due course, these things are bound to *become* antiques of value.

My family owns several typewriters, from a modern electric machine to a couple of fairly new portables. Tucked back in a closet I found a portable that must have been thirty years old. I hadn't any idea of where I had obtained that machine, but since I knew I had used it in college, I assumed it had been a secondhand gift from some relative. Because of its vintage, I assumed several people had owned it before I did.

I decided to put it in my next sale. I'm not at all sure it would have sold if I had just put it out with a low price on it. After all, how many people want an old, shaky, noisy portable typewriter when you can get a nice, new, manual portable at a discount store for a reasonable price? So I hung a large tag from the return handle and placed the machine on a crudely built pedestal. "THIS MACHINE WILL BE IN A MUSEUM IN A FEW YEARS" read the headline on the tag. Under it was this block of copy: "Last year the new Pompidou Museum in Paris had an exhibit of household and office equipment of pre–World War II vintage. It included a typewriter very much like this one. Some American museum will probably have a similar display before too long. While I wouldn't recommend that you try to type your Master's thesis on this typewriter, its near-museum-quality makes it a rare object." I had no problem getting $35 for that machine. And the man who bought it considered he had made a good long-term investment.

So don't for a minute think that because something is ancient, broken, or nonworking, it has to be thrown on the rubbish heap. Plenty of people *like* rubbish—provided it's someone else's and not their own.

11

Prior Sales: Pickers and Pests

If you read through the garage sale classifieds in your local newspaper, you will probably notice that some of them say, "No prior sales." What this means is that anyone showing up at the sale before the date and time specified in the advertisement will not be permitted to browse or purchase anything. There are pros and cons to taking this stance.

Pickers and Pests

Antiques are tough to find these days and dealers are running out of stock. Many dealers buy from people known as *pickers*. They are individuals, usually but not always known to specific dealers, who travel the countryside and find antiques by browsing through stores, visiting garage sales and country flea markets, but mostly by knocking on doors and asking people if they have any old "junk" in the attic that they would like to be rid of. There are still many unsophisticated people who don't know the antique value of some of their "junk" and are glad to sell it for a few bucks to anyone who will cart it away.

Pickers don't have stores of their own. They buy cheap and resell to the antique shops, which then mark up the merchandise still further, usually making a good profit. The picker is, in other words, the middleman between the owner of a valuable piece of "junk" and the owner of an antique shop. Under this middleman system, everyone profits and everyone is happy. Everyone, that is, except the people who run garage sales. For us, the picker can be a pain in the neck. Of course, they come in all varieties, but most of them are persistent, dogged in their determination to see what you have for sale before any other customer arrives, and relentless in their haggling. Frankly, I dislike pickers and I've tried to prevent them from making purchases prior to the legitimate opening of my sales. I think this feeling stems from an incident that occurred when I was unsophisticated and ran my first garage sale.

I was scheduled to open for business on Saturday morning at 10:00 a.m. It had rained all day Friday and, though the forecast was for a sunny weekend, Friday evening found me tired and nervous about what the morrow might bring. I was up on a ladder in my garage, trying to hang a Polynesian tapa cloth across one wall in order to provide a colorful background for some furniture pieces I planned to place in front of it. I heard a car pull into the driveway and, from my perch on the ladder, pressed the garage button to set the automatic door opener in motion. The garage door was halfway up when a couple slipped under it and greeted me with a big, "Hi, how are you?" I hadn't the foggiest notion of who they might be, but as I got down off the ladder I said, "If you're here for the sale, it doesn't begin until tomorrow at ten." The woman was already examining some items on one of the tables.

"We're just on our way through this area, en route to New Hampshire, and we won't even be in this state tomorrow, so we wondered if you'd mind if we did a little browsing while we're passing through," she said.

Though their presence was premature and I was not ready
to open shop, there seemed little I could do without being
rude and asking them to leave. I could have been firm,
absolutely firm, and said, "Sorry. Leave your name and
number and I'll let you know next time I'm having a sale—
but I am not going to sell anything before tomorrow." That's
what I *could* have done. But I was new to the game and I
figured, "The purpose of this whole operation is to dispose
of the things I have for sale . . . at a profit. What difference
does it make if these people buy it or if it's bought tomorrow
by someone else I've never set eyes on?" So I said, "Well,
OK, but I'm really not ready." I think I actually sounded
apologetic.

Luckily, I had not yet brought out any of the fine antique
items I planned to include in my sale. But hanging on a nail
in the garage was an antique wrought-iron shovel—a small
one that we used to clean out the ashes from our fireplace. It
had a lovely handle and a ring to hang it by that had been
crafted into an iron braid. It was not for sale and I had no
intention of disposing of it—at any price.

Within minutes, the male half of this team had the shovel
in his hand and was asking what I wanted for it. I told him it
was not for sale. "Oh, come on," he said. "It's exactly what
I've been looking for and I'm sure you won't miss it. Tell you
what. It's not worth it but I'll let you have two dollars for
it." I saw red. I think I felt my eyes crossing in my head.

"It's not for sale," I repeated. "It belongs to my husband.
He uses it to clean out the fireplace. He'd be upset if I sold
it." My rising anger was carefully hidden and I recall thinking that I would have to learn to deal with the public in a
gracious manner. How was I to know that most people
whom I would subsequently meet at garage sales would be
pleasant, friendly, even jolly souls, out for a bargain and a
good time—and that I wouldn't need to try very hard to be
pleasant?

But on that unforgettable occasion my first picker
whipped out two one-dollar bills and placed them on a table
near me. "You can get yourself a lovely plastic one, much

nicer than this, at Woolworth's for maybe a dollar and a half. You'll see. Your husband will be glad you sold this, and besides, we came a long distance to buy something and you wouldn't want your first customer to be disappointed, would you? Isn't it nice to begin your sale by having someone find exactly what he's been looking for?"

At that point I could have grabbed the shovel out of his hand, pushed the money back into his pocket, or ordered him off the premises. Later on, I asked myself why I hadn't at least screamed at him, "Plastic! The only plastic thing in my house is *you*—now go away and leave my shovel right where you found it!" Of course, I did no such thing. You guessed it—I let him walk out with my beautiful antique shovel and, near tears, pocketed his big-deal $2.

I later related this incident to my friend Jane Blackmar who runs the famous Blackmar Antique Shop in the heart of Connecticut's antique row, and she was able to describe the couple precisely. "Did he drive a brown Chevy station wagon?" she asked. He did. She was able to tell me the couple's name and said they were relentless pickers who could badger you nearly to distraction and that they did a very profitable business selling to dealers in that area. She had seen my shovel at my house and said that some dealer would buy it and later sell it for approximately $25.

I've gone into some detail about this incident because you should know that pickers have the ability to be hard-nosed and not at all typical of the people who will otherwise patronize your sale. Also, they can pick out all the choicest merchandise so that by the time you open to the public most of the good stuff is gone. Nonetheless, if your object is to sell everything, you might want to put up with them. Remember, though, that they will probably want you to cut prices on everything they buy. You don't get top dollar from pickers.

Other Prior Sales

There are, of course, other people who like to come to a sale before the scheduled opening. One such group of people is made up of local antique dealers and owners of second-hand furniture shops. The advantage of selling to them is that they will often buy quite a large number of objects and put you well on your way to a successful sale even before it opens officially. They like to come early because they can then spot the valuable stuff before it's carted away and because they want to be back in their own shops for their regular business day.

I can't advise you whether or not to permit prior sales to these people. My own practice is this: if I have but a handful of antiques for sale, I sell to no one before the doors open for regular business. This makes it possible for the general public to have access to my best merchandise and I think that's only fair. If someone shows up at the very beginning of a sale, he or she is entitled to get the best chance at what you have to offer.

On the other hand, when I'm running a sale for someone else and that person has quite a large number of antiques, some of them fairly expensive, I think I should exert every effort to sell them—to whomever I can. In those instances, I not only permit dealers to come the night before the sale begins; I sometimes even phone a few dealers I know well and tell them what I have that might be of special interest to them. A few dealers I know personally sometimes even buy an item over the telephone without even seeing it. They know that I won't misrepresent the condition of the item and that I will price it at a fair market value. Occasionally, the item is a piece for which they already have a customer, so they consider themselves fortunate to be able to buy it at a garage sale price.

If you're not personally acquainted with any of the antique dealers in your area, this should not stop you from calling or visiting them and mentioning the various antiques you plan to sell. As I said earlier, antique stock is hard to come by today and dealers are quite happy to get a tip on where some items might be available.

When you run your garage sale, rely on your own gut feeling in deciding whether or not to permit prior sales. If you think you can cope with dealers, if you're going to be ready to receive customers the night before or the day before the actual sale, if you're anxious about whether or not you will be able to sell those expensive antique pieces, then go ahead and allow prior sales. If not, firmly refuse to sell anything early, and stick to your resolve that no goods or money will change hands until the opening whistle has sounded.

12

Money, Money, Money—
and How to Handle It

One of the reasons you're running a garage sale is to turn your rags and other possessions into riches. And like Mr. Woolworth, you won't mind a nickel-and-dime business if in the end it adds up to big bucks. So you want to guard the proceeds, make proper change, and prevent rip-offs. Here are some tips on how to accomplish all of that, without a misstep anywhere along the way.

The Cash Box

Keep only a single main cash box. Obviously, it's easier to keep an eye on one cash container than on two or three.

The best place for your cash box is *inside your house,* behind locked doors, in the area marked, "Off Limits." While you may want to keep another cash box in the garage or elsewhere in the sale area in order to have small change nearby, it is important to limit the money in such a box to only a few dollars. If you prefer to keep the money in your pocket, do so—particularly if you're going to be wandering around a bit and don't want to leave an unattended box of cash. If you have someone specially assigned to guard the dough at a special cashier's spot, you can consider it quite safe. I don't know of anyone who has ever had the cash box stolen during a garage sale, but I am sure it has happened to someone. Even if it hasn't, this is one "first" that you don't want to be credited with.

The first rule of retailing when it comes to keeping your money safe is: keep it out of sight. The second rule is: don't create temptation. And the third is: keep as little in the cash drawer as you can—and still do business.

People who run these sales for the first time find it annoying, particularly when several customers want to pay for items at the same time, to keep running inside to make change. But you get used to it very quickly and the nuisance is outweighed by the fact that a conspicuous, unattended amount of cash can become an irresistible temptation to some people. Imagine going through all the planning, organizing, advertising, setting up, and selling—and then having someone steal all the proceeds! You'll want to strangle yourself for having been foolish enough to invite a rip-off. So do as professional retailers do: set up enough deterrents so that even determined thieves find your system impenetrable.

You might also think about limiting access to the cash box to one or, at most, two persons other than yourself. If the whole family, including some of the younger children, are permitted to take cash and make change, the chances of error increase. If you want to let the younger kids feel involved in this family happening, permit them to consummate the sale up to the point where the buyer hands them the money. Then, be sure they are taught to say, "That's a *ten*-dollar bill. I'll get your change for you." Or, "That's a *one*-dollar bill. I'll be back in a minute with your change." Then have them bring the money to *you, you* write up the receipt and enter the sale on your inventory sheet, and *you* make the change.

Mention the Amount of Money Given to You

Whether the kids are handling the transaction or you are (or Aunt Tillie or anyone else), make it a house rule that the denomination of the bill handed to the salesperson is repeated *out loud.* I am not suggesting that there are many people around who will claim that they gave you a bill larger than they actually did because they want to cheat you, though these persons do exist, and they do come to garage sales. But people are absentminded, preoccupied, or busy talking while they make payment; and frequently—more frequently than you might imagine—they truly believe they gave you a larger bill than they did. You won't offend anyone because it's a common retail practice and people are accustomed to having the clerk say, "That's two fifty out of five" or "That's six dollars out of ten." Unless you have retail experience, I know you are going to find that awkward the first few times you say it. But it will become routine and you'll soon be surprised at how naturally you mouth those words. It's a precaution. It may not be essential at your particular sale, but you never know who will show up when you invite the general public. So go by the book and you won't have any regrets.

Securing the First Day's Receipts

If you plan a two-day sale, chances are you will be so exhausted by the end of the first day that you are not going to be much in the mood to kick up your heels or dance until dawn. I don't advise planning anything social, unless your favorite niece has suddenly decided to get married that evening or you are unexpectedly asked to a party in honor of Princess Margaret. But just in case you do make a social commitment for the night of the first garage sale day, it's a good idea to arrange with your local bank to deposit the first day's proceeds into their night depository. Check with your bank and find out if it's necessary to have one of their special envelopes for such a deposit. Banks in various parts of the country have different requirements. When you make that deposit, hold out enough small bills so that you can make change the following morning when you reopen for business. If you have a weekend sale, your bank will be closed Sunday and some cash on hand is essential. So don't put it all in the night depository.

If your bank doesn't have such a night deposit arrangement—and most do—*don't* go out at the end of the first sale day, no matter what. Stay home and send someone downtown for a take-home pizza or other fast food. You're going to be too tired to prepare dinner—I guarantee it. We will go into that subject more fully in the chapter on feeding the troops.

Should You Accept Checks?

There is always a risk in accepting a check from someone you don't know and whom you will probably never see again. But it is a calculated risk. After all, passing a bad check is illegal and even dishonest people know that such a deliberate act is more than a misdemeanor in most states. However, it takes only a single bad check, if it's for a large enough amount, to spoil your whole garage sale. So you need to be cautious.

Of course, you can make it a cash-only sale, but most people don't carry enough cash with them to pay for furniture or appliances or for anything that runs upward of $40 or $50. This means you could conceivably lose out on some sales of big-ticket items. My own experience has been that a few cautions, observed religiously and without exception, will minimize the risk involved in taking checks. Here's how to handle checks, should you decide to accept them.

1. Accept no checks for purchases under $10.

Make this a sale policy and put up a sign to this effect so that customers don't feel they are being discriminated against when you ask them for cash.

2. Ask for a driver's license as identification.

A driver's license that hasn't expired is the best form of identification. If your sale is in a city where some people don't drive, two charge cards (be sure that at least one has an address as well as signature on it), a Social Security card, or a bank card with a photo or signature will usually tell you that the person is who he or she claims to be.

Beware of expired licenses and expired credit cards. They could signify that the license or card was picked out of a trash basket.

3. Be sure to check the signature.

Look at the signature on the check. Look at the signature on the identification you have been offered. If they don't look at all alike, ask for additional identification. Copying down the license plate number of a purchaser's car is an excellent way to prevent fraud. Unless a car has been stolen—and I think that for our purposes we can eliminate that consideration, because people just don't steal cars and go to garage sales—a license number makes it possible for the police to check out its ownership in minutes should stealth or fraud be suspected. But I think this measure may be too extreme for the average garage sale.

4. Ask for an address and phone number.

If this information is not already printed on the check, request an address and phone number and write both on the check. Sometimes, perfectly honorable people will accidentally and unwittingly overdraw their checking accounts. If the check is returned to you marked "insufficient funds," and if you have the person's number, you can call and politely mention what has happened. This has occurred a few times at some of my garage sales and each time the person was very apologetic, assured me that a deposit had been or would be made, and asked me to redeposit the check. None of those ever bounced twice.

If you fail to take down the person's address and phone number, and something like this occurs, you will have difficulty getting the buyer's bank to tell you how to reach the person. The chances are excellent that you are never going to need to reach any of the people who come to your sale and pay by check. Despite what you may read in the papers, most people *are* both honest and honorable. Nonetheless, better cautious than sorry.

If you think you would rather not handle checks because of the nuisance and the risks involved, be sure that you write in your advertisement and flyers: "CASH AND CARRY ONLY." Also display a prominent sign at your sale that says, "SORRY, WE CAN'T ACCEPT CHECKS. ALL SALES ARE CASH ONLY." You might want to add this footnote: "A small deposit will hold any article until you can cash your own check at your bank."

Opening Up with Cash

After your sale has been going on for a couple of hours, you will have plenty of coins and small bills with which to make change. But you are going to need some money on hand when you open for business, so plan to visit the bank the day before the opening and withdraw a small amount of cash. Keep a record of what you started with so that you can subtract it from your total take at the end of the day in order to know exactly how much you profited.

My suggestion is that you open with a roll of quarters ($10), two rolls of dimes ($10), two rolls of nickels ($4), twenty one-dollar bills ($20) and five five-dollar bills ($25).

Here's a procedure I always follow. I remove my investment money (the cash I started out with), from the kitty as my proceeds start to mount up. If I have a couple of hundred dollars on hand, I withdraw the, say, $69 I began with and put it in my pocketbook, inside the house, or in some very safe hiding place. This procedure ensures that you do not get confused about how much the sale has grossed, and it also makes the cash box easier to handle as it fills up with the day's proceeds.

13

Security: Preventing Rip-Offs

I am sorry to report that the rip-off artists of the world have learned about garage sales. That doesn't mean there are dishonest people lurking around every corner, just waiting to steal your money or your goods. But unless you live in a truly small town where everyone knows everyone else, it is possible that someone visiting your sale might walk away without paying for the merchandise he or she is carrying off. It has happened to me, and in a town of only 30,000 people—not really a large town. A woman walked off wearing a lovely Bergdorf Goodman raincoat I had put up for sale and carrying a stunning evening bag. When I discovered these items were missing, two friends helping me with the sale remembered seeing the woman with both items, and neither friend had received payment for them. Nor had either one considered it strange that someone in a raincoat on a warm, sunny afternoon would be carrying a dressy evening bag. Both assumed she was wearing her own coat and that she had picked up the bag to examine it. Besides, they were too busy at that moment to do more than glance in the woman's direction. In any event, the loss of these two pieces of merchandise wiped out more than $50 of my profit that day and left me with a good deal of anger.

Other garage sale specialists have told me of people loading furniture in their station wagons, who, when questioned, merely stated they were purchasing the furniture and would be right back to make payment. And some sellers have found that small items, such as jewelry, are often unaccounted for at the end of the sale.

Minimizing Risk

There are a number of things you can do to minimize the possibility of anyone getting something for nothing—this is, after all, a sale, not a giveaway.

First, everyone helping you (your staff) should have a pretty good grasp of what is up for sale, which areas are sale areas and which are off limits, and what system you plan to use to keep track of sold merchandise. Before you open your door to customers, take your assistants on a quick tour of the premises, indicating what is included in your inventory. Use the opportunity to give them a bit of information about certain items that might draw inquiries.

Next, close and, if possible, *lock* all doors leading to nonsale areas. Post signs on these doors saying: "PLEASE DO NOT ENTER. NO SALE ITEMS BEYOND THIS DOOR." Don't worry that someone might consider such an edict unfriendly. Better unfriendly than unwary. Honest people will understand. You don't have to worry about the other kind.

The best way to prevent rip-offs is to make it obvious to strangers that someone is watching. Never, under any circumstances, permit a stranger to remain in a room unattended. Here is one of the most common tricks practiced by people who visit antique shops for the purpose of stealing. Two or more people, working together, enter the premises and, while one diverts the attention of the shop owner by expressing interest in and asking a number of questions about an item in a distant corner of the store or in a second room, the accomplice seizes the opportunity to walk out with something or perhaps slip a small item into a pocket or purse. So, if you plan to have more than one room with sale merchandise, be certain that someone is in each room whenever a customer enters it.

I have a young teenage nephew who stands six feet two inches tall and weighs 185 pounds. I always get him to help out at my garage sales. He does a bit of the heavy lugging of items, carries big pieces to customers' cars, but mostly what he does is just stand around and look like he is observing the action. With his arms folded across his tight-fitting jersey, he looks every bit like a New York nightclub bouncer and, though he has a nice, country boy smile on his face, you get the impression that he is aware of everything going on. He is. If there aren't any big young men in your family who can play this role at your sale, someone else—big or small, male or female—can make customers aware of surveillance by commenting (preferably with a smile and a friendly tone of voice) about the merchandise being examined: "That was my grandmother's china; she brought it with her from Europe." "Is there a price tag on that? I don't know whether Mother marked it or not." "We have two of those if you're interested; the other one is in the garage." "Most of these men's suits are size 40 regular, but a few of them are 42." A bit of friendly conversation can let the browser know that she or he is not alone.

Inventory Control

The best way to keep an inventory control is also the hardest way, and not everyone is willing to go to the trouble. Personally, I think it's worth it.

Make a master list of every item for sale. Use a legal-size pad. Have four columns on each page in addition to the column listing the items. The second column is for the price you have put on the tag. The third column is blank. You use it only if you decide to mark down an item during the course of your sale. When that happens, cross out the original price and write in the new one. The fourth column is where you write in the price *received* for the item when it is actually sold. And the fifth column is for the initials of the person who takes the money for that transaction.

This could be a time-consuming procedure. If you have a hundred or more items in your sale, the person taking the money has to go down the long list to find the item and record the receipt of payment. One way to get around this is to list only items that are $10 or more and just leave blank pages for lower-priced goods to be listed as they are sold. When such an inexpensive item goes, the person taking the money merely scribbles down on the blank sheets a descriptive phrase to identify the piece, along with her or his initials and the price paid.

Jewelry Protection

Jewelry and other small, precious items should be kept at the checkout table, where you want to have someone posted or seated at all times. Small jewelry pieces and such things as silver spoons have a way of vanishing. Keep an eye peeled!

While it is much rarer to have someone arrive at your sale with a large shopping bag than it is in a retail store, where customers may be doing a round of shopping and bringing in purchases they just made elsewhere, it does happen. Since there is no logical reason for anyone to arrive carrying such a bag—it can be left in the car—I always ask customers to place bags at the checkout desk for safekeeping. I phrase it as a suggestion, not an order, to avoid hurt feelings: "Here . . . may I put your shopping bag under the counter so it won't latch on to anything and accidentally break something?" Or, "We've set aside a space right here to leave all shopping bags." As I said before regarding locked doors, the honest people understand. And the others justify your precautions.

Sales Receipts

Another effective system in preventing rip-offs is to hand each purchaser a sales slip (receipt) and state, "You will need it when you leave." Even if you don't have a husky nephew standing guard in your driveway, the knowledge that customers might be asked for their receipts on the way out has a way of deterring stealth. Be quite obvious about making these receipts.

Your sales slips can be as simple as the sort of check you get when you have a cup of coffee in a drugstore or luncheonette. Buy a couple of pads of such receipts where you buy your price tags and other sale supplies. Then, when you are paid for an article, write the name of the item on the slip, the amount paid for it, and in large letters scribble "PAID" along with your initials. Hand it to the customer with the change and with your friendly "Thank you very much," or "So glad you were able to find something you like," or "I know you're going to enjoy using it." This combines friendliness and a bit of appreciation with the implication that receipts might be called for when the goods are placed in the customer's car.

The chapter on handling money has already told you how to handle checks, should you decide to accept them in lieu of cash for major large-ticket items. You also now know how to secure your cash box by keeping most of the money locked up inside your house, in areas not open to the public. Of course, all the preventive techniques and systems aren't as good as your own alertness and having enough staff on hand to keep watch when you are occupied with a customer. Unless you plan to have a one-room sale and never leave the room, be sure you can count on family or friends to help you run your big event.

14

Making People Feel Comfortable in Your Store

If you've been to many garage sales, you know they range from depressing to terrific. Much of your enjoyment depends on the way the people running the sale react to your presence. And their behavior will, in turn, determine yours, including whether or not you buy anything or just walk out quickly, feeling sorry that you bothered to come.

Sales fall into certain basic categories: (1) those that spill over with friendliness in terms of the proprietor's behavior and his or her pleasure in seeing you; (2) those in which the sellers are proper but aloof, often because they're not sure exactly how friendly they should be and because they want to avoid what might seem like high-pressure salesmanship; (3) those in which a couple of adults sit in a corner conversing among themselves with total disregard and no open acknowledgment of the people who have come to browse and buy. Another version of this latter sale is to be found where no adult is in evidence and a couple of youngsters are minding the store. One sometimes even gets the impression that the sale is being run for the kids, so that they can pick up a few dollars by selling their broken old roller skates and their jigsaw puzzles with half the pieces missing. Please don't have that kind of a sale. It depresses the whole industry.

If you're going to have a garage sale, run it properly. Be nice. Be friendly. You don't have to gush over customers, but neither do you have to act like you wish you had never gotten into the whole thing in the first place and that the lepers would do you a favor if they wouldn't contaminate your estate by stepping foot inside your garage.

Naturally, your own personality will have a great deal to do with the way you handle prospective buyers. I'm not suggesting that you try to change your personal style for the purpose of this special event. But all of us have quotients of charm and graciousness that we display in different quantities with different people, depending on the relationship. I am suggesting that, without indulging in inappropriate and phony delight at the sight of a customer, you do make an attempt to display the more gracious side of your personality. With this in mind, here are some dos and don'ts on correct behavior for the proprietor of a garage sale.

Don't ignore people who show up. To do so is to make people feel that you are so aloof you consider yourself superior to these bargain hunters.

Do acknowledge someone's arrival. It is sufficient to say, "Good morning" or "Hi" and "Come right in and look around." This indicates that you're aware of the prospect's presence and want to make him or her welcome.

Do offer information if someone is looking at an item that might have a history or a special sales point.

Don't, on the other hand, go into lengthy and uninvited detail. You will surely give the impression that you're pushing too hard and will very likely scare the prospective buyer into moving on. Let me give you an example. A woman arrives at your sale with a teenage daughter. The daughter immediately goes to the rack of garments you've put up for sale. Her mother wanders over to a table of old dishes and glasses. The girl starts to examine an old ankle-length silk nightgown that you bought in Florence, Italy, many years ago but never wore. You might, after greeting the customer, say casually, "Isn't that lovely? You'll notice that it's all handmade, including the lace around the top." Enough! You've given her something to look at and think about. Now walk away. Permit her to spend as much time as she wants with that garment. Let her think it over. Let her hold it up against herself and stand in front of the mirror. (You might have added, "There's a mirror in the corner if you want to hold it up and see how it looks.")

Again, don't go on and on: "You know, my husband and I were in Florence—Italy, you know? And we came across this absolutely marvelous shop right off the Ponte Vecchio on the Arno River, you know? And I simply had to have that nightgown, it was so beautifully made. So I brought it back with me and, would you believe it, I found it almost too lovely to wear. I kept it in tissue paper all these years. It's a great buy at that price, too. I'm sure you'd find it soft and comfortable to sleep in." Well, chances are this young miss doesn't sleep in long, silk nighties and that she is interested in the garment as an evening dress. Maybe she's thinking of wearing it to her friend's wedding in the woods, which is coming up soon. You're just scaring her away by implying that this is a nightgown and everyone will know it's a nightgown. She may also feel she doesn't want a woman older than she is to tell her what's nice—she has her own ideas.

So be observant. Look like you're ready to supply information if wanted. But don't carry on ad infinitum about any particular item unless a customer specifically asks you questions about it. Conversely, don't act so disinterested that you give the impression you wish people wouldn't touch your precious possessions.

Consider Providing Refreshments

Do consider offering some refreshment. This could be a

large pot of iced tea—or coffee, if you can stand the expense—with paper cups and a small sign saying, "Have some tea on us and thank you for coming." If you don't want to cope with refilling the tea urn or coffeepot, you can set out a very large bowl of popcorn with a similar sign. But don't butter the corn; you don't want sticky fingers touching your merchandise. Small, dry pretzel sticks, or any of the less expensive and nongreasy party snacks at your supermarket are also good. They help people relax and encourage them to stay longer, which usually promotes additional purchases. Be sure that you don't put out any refreshments that are messy—and no lollipops. Remember to provide a trash receptacle nearby for used cups and wrappers.

Do determine in advance that you are going to take a firm stand on the matter of children touching the merchandise. You can't stop people from bringing the kids; if you did, you would be eliminating a large number of families. But you can post a sign that says, "PLEASE DO NOT LET YOUR CHILDREN HANDLE THE ITEMS . . . IF ONE OF THEM BREAKS SOMETHING, CONSIDER THAT YOU'VE BOUGHT IT." I know that this may seem a bit harsh, but the other side of the coin is that being a softy where small children are concerned could mean a substantial loss even if only one important piece is broken. Also think about the danger of a small child pulling down a draping cloth from a table and being hurt in the process, or possibly stepping on a rake or picking up a pair of garden shears.

Retailers will tell you that a firm comment, when accompanied by a smile and a pleasant tone of voice, takes the edge off your remark and offends no one. I am not advising you to say, "Get that hare-brained monster away from the lawn mower!" Just say, "I think it would be better if your little girl sat over there on the lawn instead of on the lawn mower. She can watch the birds on the feeder." Mom will get the message.

15

How to Run
an Apartment House Sale

The ordinary household garage sale is a much more common occurrence in suburban communities where people live in private homes than it is in big cities. One reason is that the grounds of a private residence permit ample space for this type of activity. The second reason is, alas, that urban areas have higher crime rates and people in cities are less inclined to let just anyone off the street amble into their apartments.

However, there are ways to minimize risk and put some limit on the clientele you invite to your happening. In the East, I have managed some apartment sales that have gone off without a hitch and chalked up enormous profits. If no one in your apartment house has ever had such a sale, and if you want to run one, go ahead and be the first one on your block. If nothing else, the novelty of the event is sure to attract enough customers to make it worth the effort.

Limiting the Clientele

The very first apartment house sale I ever handled was in a complex of four buildings, each of which had between 300 and 400 units. If I had notified the residents of all four buildings about the event, approximately 1,500 households would have known about it. On that occasion, I didn't think we could handle big crowds because the sale was to be held in a three-room apartment and the walking-around space was limited. My client and I made the decision to invite only the people in the building in which her apartment was situated and to post a few additional signs in the laundry rooms of the other three buildings, just to catch a bit of outside traffic. It turned out to be more than enough.

Depending on the size of your apartment house, you should decide at the outset whether you want to tell only the people in your building about the sale or publicize it elsewhere as well. Limiting the announcements offers a means of screening your customers, albeit a superficial means. After all, if the people live in your building, you probably have at least a nodding acquaintance with most of them. In addition, before any person or family was rented (or sold) an apartment, some sort of screening by the management probably took place. So, through such built-in restrictions you have cut your risk to an acceptable minimum.

If, however, there aren't enough tenants in your own building to assure you of sufficient traffic, consider extending notice of the sale to one or two other good apartment houses on your street or in the immediate vicinity. Don't go beyond that. You won't need to.

Spreading the Word

Telling people about an apartment sale calls for techniques different from those used for similar events held in private suburban homes. While the latter lean heavily on local newspaper ads, the apartment sale uses the flyer as the principal announcement. (See Chapter 9.)

The way you distribute your flyer is your control over who knows about the event. You most certainly want to avoid a newspaper ad, which broadcasts word of the happening to all sorts of people, some of whom you might not particularly want to cross your doorstep.

In apartment sales, flyers are distributed apartment by apartment and are posted in strategic heavy-traffic areas. How many such areas are available to you depends on the building's rules and regulations. Only in a small number of residential buildings will anyone stop you from slipping a single-sheet flyer under the door of each apartment. Where the postman is friendly, I have had good luck in getting him to include a folded flyer (don't expect him to fold them for you) with each tenant's mail on a specified day. And on the very few occasions where I haven't been able to manage this, I obtained permission from the building management or superintendent to tack up, near the letter boxes, a small cardboard box or manila envelope holding the flyers, on which I had printed the words "TENANTS—PLEASE TAKE ONE." Under such circumstances, the box or envelope has to be refilled a couple of times as the flyers dwindle in number. Curiosity is a wonderful sales tool. Hardly any tenant can resist taking a notice out of a container when specifically invited to do so. Between the flyer box, the helpful postman, and slipping notices under doors (or under door handles or knobs), it is possible to notify everyone in the chosen buildings about the upcoming event.

Posting in High Traffic Areas

You also want to be certain to post copies of your flyer in the laundry room, if your building has one, or in any other on-premise location that enjoys a great deal of traffic, such as the package room, the public telephone booth area, the place where baby carriages and bicycles are stored, the building garage, and so on.

The very best place to post your flyer is in each of the building's elevators. However, this is also the most difficult place to put them, since many buildings explicitly forbid such postings. If there is no such regulation in your own apartment house, seize the opportunity. You will have a captive audience for your message, coming and going.

Some buildings that do not allow elevator posting do have furniture in the lobbies and it is often possible to arrange with the doorman for a stack of flyers to be left on one of the tables with a homemade paperweight on top of the stack that reads: "TAKE ONE, PLEASE." Most doormen and superintendents, if you cross their palms with green, will be agreeable to picking up the discarded flyers, should there be any. Even in these inflationary times, a ten-dollar bill will work wonders in getting cooperation from the building's maintenance personnel. Don't consider this a bribe. As long as you aren't asking someone to break a rule—and no amount of money will get an elevator man to post a sign in an elevator if building rules prohibit it—look on it as an extra service you are requesting, on a one-time basis, for which you are willing to pay.

Of course, if you're rich enough to live in an apartment house which is so elegant that no sale would be condoned by anyone, at any level, then you're probably rich enough to give all your goodies to charity and skip the sale. Or you can rename the event and make it a cocktail party, inviting everyone in the building to come. You would then want your invitation to explain the purpose of the party and state that admission would be "By Invitation Only." I, myself, have never gone the cocktail party route, but why not? If Lauren Bacall were to invite me to sell her castaway clothes and furniture in her apartment at the Dakota, that is precisely the type of event I would recommend.

When to Make Your Announcement

If your sale will take place on the weekend or on Friday and Saturday, the best day to distribute the notices is Wednesday. This allows sufficient advance notice so interested people can plan a short visit to your apartment. And it isn't so far ahead of the activity that people will forget it.

If you're planning a spring or summer sale when many apartment house dwellers go to the country or the shore for the weekend, you should give a lot of thought to having a midweek event. Running an apartment sale a few hours in the morning and a couple in the evening, on Tuesday, Wednesday, and Thursday, is likely to bring in all the customers you will need. In such cases, I have my notices in everybody's box or under their doors on the Monday of the sale week. Flyers posted on bulletin boards and elsewhere can go up the previous week.

Apartment Sale Hours Can Be Staggered

Since you're not going to be moving a lot of stuff out of the apartment as you would if you were running the event in a garage or a driveway, and since people won't be traveling long distances—at most they will be taking a turn around the block or going up or down in an elevator—you have a wider choice of sale hours. You can, for example, have a two-day sale with the hours listed as 9:00 a.m. to 11:00 a.m. and 4:00 p.m. to 7:00 p.m. This gives both homemakers and people working outside the home a good choice of hours when they can be accommodated. And it doesn't tie you in to the apartment for a seven- or eight-hour stretch. However, if you do go the route of such a split-session sale, be certain that when you go out you put a notice on your door stating precisely when you will once again be open for business. Lots of people aren't careful readers, or they are forgetful. You can count on having some callers during the nonsale hours.

Smaller Sales Area May Not Indicate Smaller Sales Staff

The rule about not having people enter your home (see chapters 8 and 13) obviously goes out the window when it comes to apartment sales. Your apartment is where it's all at. However, you should consider closing off the bedroom if there is no large piece of furniture for sale in that room. Certainly your bathroom should carry the "PLEASE DO NOT ENTER—PRIVATE" sign so that you have at least one room where no strangers are permitted to go. In that room you will want to hide your cash box, and I mean *hide* it. If anyone asks to use your bathroom, just say you are sorry but it's out of order, or make some other excuse. After all, they probably live in your building or very nearby—let them go home and then come back again if the sale items interest them. Your graciousness as a shopkeeper need not extend to sharing your bathroom with strangers.

However, even if your money is cached in an off-limits room, you still want to have someone assist you in each of the other sale rooms. If there are two rooms of merchandise, someone has to hold down the fort in each of those rooms. And there should definitely be someone standing or sitting near the entrance to the apartment. He or she can serve as official greeter and official checker to see that nothing that hasn't been paid for is waltzing into the corridor. Enough said!

For security reasons, don't let anyone into your apartment after the sale has closed for the day and your door is bolted shut. You are probably going to have quite a bit of cash and checks on hand and some unknown person arriving after hours should be told to come back the next day when the sale reopens. Don't worry about disappointing anyone. Be firm. Closed is closed.

Getting Sold Merchandise Out of the Apartment

When you run a garage sale to which people come by car, they're prepared to cart off their purchases as they leave the premises. However, someone at an apartment sale who buys a sofa or a bed or an item too heavy or bulky to be carted off by one individual may have a bit of a problem applying your cash-and-carry edict. Still, you are going to want to give that buyer every possible aid in taking home the item that was bought.

One thing you can do is talk to the building handyman or superintendent before the first sale day and explain what's going on. Ask him if he would be available to help another tenant, whoever it may turn out to be, move some big piece of furniture to the buyer's apartment in exchange for a reasonable fee or tip. If he agrees, and there is a good likelihood he will, explain to the purchaser that he is willing to help move the piece for a specified amount. The buyer should expect to pay the moving fee or get one of his or her friends to pitch in and cart it to its new home. You should not be expected to pay any carting expense.

If the purchaser of a large-ticket item wants to come back with a friend or spouse on a subsequent day to pick up some item, be sure the arrangements you make are very specific as to the day and hour when they will come. And ask for full payment the day the sale is consummated. If the item isn't paid for, the customer might have a change of mind, your sale will be over, and you will be left holding the merchandise. So have buyers pay now, pick up merchandise later if they must, but find out exactly when they will call for it. Also exchange phone numbers in case either of you has to change the plan. And if you aren't acquainted with the buyer, have someone keep you company in your apartment at the time the piece is to be picked up.

Disposing of Unsold Merchandise

People who are giving up their apartments and moving to homes elsewhere often want to redecorate to suit the new place. If you're one of these people, you may want to dispose of all but very personal possessions when you run your sale. Should you find at the end of the first day that you still have a number of items in which there is not too much interest, you would be well advised to cut the prices or mark them: "Name your price. No reasonable offer refused." (For more on setting prices, see Chapter 6.)

If you have lots of books and records that don't seem to be moving, and if they're items you truly don't want to cart to your next residence, put a sign on the book and record table that reads: "With purchase over $10 you can have a book or record, *free!*" This will save you the trouble and expense of boxing and moving things you really would like to get rid of.

If you are still unable to unload every last bit of merchandise, call the Salvation Army, Goodwill Industries, or any of the other local charities in your area and tell them what merchandise you would like to donate. They will tell you whether it is of interest to them and will arrange a mutually convenient time to pick up the items that are too large or too heavy for you to bring to their store. They will then send you a paper verifying the fact that you contributed the specified merchandise and stating its value. Attaching a copy of this statement to your income tax return will allow you to list the total donation as a charitable contribution for that year. And you will have a nice, empty apartment if you plan to move, or a very neat one if you're just doing your spring cleaning.

Apartment sales, carefully planned and managed, can be very rewarding and can involve a comparatively small amount of preparation and work. By drawing your customers from a limited circle and planning your hours to accommodate both those who work at home and those who work outside, there is no reason why your own sale should not be safe, successful, and a tribute to your organizational skills as well as to your ability to turn rags into riches.

16

The Joint Sale

Frequently, people who feel they don't have quite enough merchandise to run a successful garage sale, or others who can't face the job of running one alone, band together and conduct a joint sale. This has both advantages and disadvantages and some advice and cautions are in order.

The principal advantage, of course, is to the customer, who almost always prefers to find a big choice and a wide variety of items when attending a sale. The other main advantage is that there are more hands available to talk to customers, handle transactions, keep watch over cash and jewelry, and generally share in the work and fun.

The principal disadvantage is that friction can arise between the venture partners if arrangements aren't well worked out in advance.

Sharing a Philosophy, Sharing the Work

Nothing will break up a longstanding friendship quicker

than a cooperative venture in which one partner fails to cooperate. Sometimes, however, such seeming lack of cooperation is not willful but due to the fact that someone doesn't fully understand what is expected of her or him.

In the interest of a good sale, your friendship, and your sanity, have a long, serious, detailed conversation with the person joining you in this activity before you agree to make it a cooperative venture. In such a preliminary conversation, you may learn that you two are really not suited to each other—as retailers, that is.

One of the things you should share, though it is not critical to the operation, is a pricing philosophy. If one partner expects to ask high prices, it could make customers feel that *all* the prices are high. This could have a negative effect on the sale of your own merchandise and turn off some customers. You should also have a clear understanding on whether you plan to make this a jumble-and-junk presentation or one that combines some inexpensive items with a number of useful and valuable ones. And you should have an agreement on whether you are going to dress up your displays with tablecloths or skirts or just dump everything every which way. You should talk about whose family members will help at the sale, who will post flyers around town, who will put up road signs, and who will help clean up when the sale is over. Don't overlook this last important consideration.

None of these things should be left to chance. Don't end the conversation with your would-be partner on a note of "let's wait and see." If you go into this activity with the attitude that things will somehow work themselves out and that you will both resolve the problems as they come along, you're going to end up with one big headache and maybe even one big fight.

Settle everything in advance. You are not going to have time on the sale days to have any meaningful discussions. Things will be moving too fast and exhaustion sometimes leads to frayed tempers. You are forewarned!

Moving the Goods to the Sale Site

Don't plan to move one person's possessions to the site of the garage sale at the last minute. You may find out too late that you haven't enough display tables, that you have neglected to make necessary signs, and that some of the larger pieces might not fit where you thought they would. All goods should certainly be on the premises at least one day before you open for business. If you can manage to keep your cars out of the garage for a few days, it's even better to get everything into one location two or three days ahead of the event. You're asking for disaster if you count on moving in your partner's merchandise the morning that you open for business.

There is another reason for such advance movement of goods. If half of the joint sale team is busy moving in his or her possessions practically until day one, that person is not going to have much time to contribute a fair share in doing all the other things that need to be done the day before you open. Good advance planning, down to the last detail, is essential when a cooperative endeavor is under way.

Handling the Receipts

Handling the receipts at a joint sale calls for some special arrangements, and these should also be determined in advance. You have a choice of two methods.

One is to have absolutely separate sale areas for each venture partner. That is the flea market method of operation. Each party has space for showing goods, including some display tables, and handles his or her own transactions. Money taken in at each sale site is kept by the person who owns that part of the inventory.

The alternative is to have different-colored tags and different inventory lists, and each transaction is then credited to the person whose possession it is. This technique is fraught with possibilities of error but it does have the advantage of all hands working for the overall good of the sale and not having to say, "Sorry, that item isn't mine. Ask the lady over there in the paisley dress." The not-my-table attitude can put off some customers.

By keeping a running inventory list, as discussed earlier, you decrease the possibility of crediting the wrong partner with a sale. Since your inventory will list every large item, as well as who sold it and how much was paid for it, you can always go back over the list when the event is finished and check for possible mistakes.

Much, of course, will depend on the closeness of the friendship between you and your partner, how long you have known each other, and how efficient each of you is. If you are superefficient, I would not recommend that you go into a joint venture with someone you consider scatterbrained or unlikely to be able to handle retail transactions. You will soon find yourself taking over all of the work and growing increasingly irritated as you watch your partner totally disregard the procedures you set up for such things as handling cash, issuing receipts, and recording items sold.

Beware the would-be partner who agrees, in principle, to run a joint sale with you but can never find the time to get together in order to discuss plans, dates, assignments, etc. If one partner takes the activity seriously and intends to realize some meaningful return from it, and if the other partner considers it a great big lark that can be thrown together at the last moment, you may be mismatched. Break up the engagement before you tie the knot. Seek another partner or go it alone.

On the other hand, if you and your potential partner have the same sale philosophy and are mutually supportive, having a fifty-fifty relationship can ease the burden of the preparatory work and offer you someone with whom you can share a chuckle when things are going well. And a groan, should it rain on your parade.

17

Feeding the Troops: How Not to Starve During Your Sale

If your sale is a bomb and no one comes, you're going to be too depressed to eat. But I see that as extremely unlikely if you follow the merchandising tips and the advertising and posting advice in this book—unless, of course, there is an unexpected tornado or flood the day of your happening.

We know that your sale is going to be a terrific neighborhood event and the money is going to roll in and there will be periods when you won't have time to go to the bathroom. Certainly there will be no period when you can be absolutely sure that no customers are about to arrive—no such period when you can put up a sign saying, "Out to Lunch." So you had better be prepared to eat on the run for the two or more days of your activity.

Making Do without Breakfast

I don't care how much preorganizing you have done, how

long in advance you began to get ready for the grand opening. There are simply so many things that can't be done until just before you open for business that the first morning won't allow enough time for a sit-down breakfast. If you know this in advance, you will set out your breakfast makings the night before the curtain goes up. Then you can grab a cup of whatever, or a bowl of something, or a slice of toast, while you are moving around. Keep in mind that you can't move display tables outside or set them up with merchandise until the morning of the sale. If you were to do it the night before, unexpected rain or dew could present you with some soggy display counters.

On page 138 is a list of things to do the morning of the first day. When you examine this list, you will understand why I'm telling you that the night before you should also lay out the clothes you plan to wear. You're going to be moving very fast when that alarm clock goes off.

Forget Diets, Hot Food, and Good Manners

As far as eating is concerned, it's going to be catch as catch can. The day before you open, prepare some tuna salad, or bring in and cut up a barbecued chicken from the deli, or make a casserole or other dish that doesn't need to be reheated. On the sale days, you're not going to have time to wash lettuce for a salad, to cut up vegetables, or even to heat a can of soup. Trust me, I know what I'm talking about.

Tell the family that there will be no regular meal hours during the sale period. All family members—big and little—help themselves when hungry. Plenty of bread and rolls for quickly made sandwiches are good, as are cookies or no-mess cakes, things that might usually be tabu in your house. Milk, premixed iced tea, soft drinks, fruit juice—anything that requires no on-the-spot preparation, and preferably is consumable in disposable cups, is permissible. You can go back to counting calories and avoiding junk foods when things return to normal after the sale.

What is essential is to remember to eat *something* during the day, no matter that you might have to consume it a bite at a time whenever you go inside to the cash box. If you don't eat, you are likely to become irritable, which would be disastrous. Remember, you are going to be a gracious, charming host or hostess to your customers and browsers. So eat when you can and what you can, but not so large a quantity that you feel you want to go upstairs and take a nap.

No Liquor, Beer, or Wine during Sale Hours

Whatever your ordinary alcoholic consumption may be, you should refrain from such drinking anything during sale hours. That also goes for everyone helping you with the sale. If it's a hot day and you've done a lot of rushing around, a cold beer might sound like a good idea when it's offered to you. Decline the offer. There are two reasons for this advice. First, some people might not like the idea of transacting business with someone who smells of beer or gin. You might say, "That's *their* problem, not mine," but you would be wrong. Without taking sides, I have to point out a fact of life to you: in retailing, the customer is always right. If you know it might cost you one or more sales, you will probably be willing to forgo the afternoon libation. You can have your drink or drinks when the customers go home and you close up for the evening.

The second reason why alcoholic beverages and retailing don't mix is that you increase the chance of error in making change. You've done a lot of work to put this event together. You want to get every dollar out of it that you can reasonably expect. Don't accidentally give away the profit on an item by returning too much change. You will be growing increasingly tired as the day wears on and you're going to need to be constantly alert. Anything that dulls your senses, whether it be overeating or consuming alcohol, is ill advised. You want to look sharp, feel sharp, be sharp.

So when you're close to the sale, and you're making a list of things to do before opening day, be sure to list the preparation of cold, nonspoiling food dishes and the purchase of some snack items. Forget the six-pack of beer.

Best of all, if you have any friends who ask you, "Is there anything I can do to help?" say "Yes. How would you like to bring over some of your wonderful potato salad, or one of your marvelous cold noodle puddings? I know my family will be forever grateful to you."

After all, isn't that what friends are for?

18

Ten Questions Frequently Asked by Garage Sale Operators

1. Where should I be when I open for business?

You should set up one spot that will be your cash desk or command post or headquarters—call it what you like. This is *your* place unless you choose to assign it to one of your helpers. At this command post you will need a desk or table on which to keep a supply of extra tags, safety pins, masking tape, marking pencils, shirt cardboards for new signs that might become necessary after you open, and receipt pads. You will also want to have some newspapers and string for wrapping and a supply of grocery bags. And don't forget an ashtray so that you can ask customers to put out their cigarettes before entering the garage.

You will also display your jewelry and small expensive items on one part of this table, where you or one of your helpers can keep an eye on such merchandise. Your secondary cash box—the one containing only small change and a handful of single bills (most of your money is going to be hidden inside, behind locked doors)—will also be at this post. This is where you should be when you open for business. After a few hours you will undoubtedly be grateful that you remembered to put a chair at this desk—with a tag on it reading, "THIS CHAIR IS NOT FOR SALE." Without that tag, you might find it being carted off from under you.

2. What should I do if someone tries to bargain, tries to get an item for less than the price on the tag?

Haggling is part of the game. Some people enjoy bargaining and you must not be put off or offended by it. There are many people who enjoy garage sales much more if they can get the sale operator to cut the price, even if only by a few cents.

Experienced hagglers usually start by asking, "Is this the best you can do on this item?" or "Can you possible do a bit better on this price?" If you really don't want to sell it for less, say so in a nice, friendly way: "That's about as low as I can go on that. If I can't get that much out of it I think I'll just hang on to it for a while." However, if you think you would be willing to part with the item for a bit less, then say so, mentioning the lowered price. You can phrase it this way so that the haggler is satisfied with your reply: "Well, I did think that was a fair price, but if you want it I'll take $2 (or whatever) off the ticket price for you."

Don't sigh or groan or exchange glances with one of your helpers when someone asks for a better price. If you are courteous, most hagglers will be good-natured about accepting the fact that a price is as low as you are prepared to go. And, if they truly want an item, chances are good that tney will buy it at the stated price.

3. Are garage sales legal everywhere?

I never heard of any town that prohibits such sales,

though it is possible that such prohibitions do exist. Many towns, however, do require you to obtain a permit for an event of this type. The purpose of this is not to discourage your garage sale but to prevent people from running so many sales at the same address that they are virtually conducting a year-round retail business from their homes—often an illegal practice where there are strict residential zoning laws. In some towns you are permitted to have no more than two garage sales each year at the same address.

There are also places where special ordinances prohibit the posting of signs in specific areas and require you to remove your signs when your sale is over—something you should do whether the law requires it or not.

To be on the safe side, call your local police department or zoning board and ask whether there are any special requirements or prohibitions. You may have to pay a permit fee, but this is never more than a couple of dollars. It isn't that the town is trying to find a new source of revenue. The fee requirement is usually in effect so that the town management has an opportunity to hand you, or mail to you, a copy of the local regulations.

4. Will I be expected to wrap merchandise?

Most customers at a garage sale don't expect you to wrap their purchases. It is part of the tradition of such sales that people walk out carrying the oddest things in their hands—they almost seem to be proudly displaying to others they meet on the way in, the wonderful treasures they were smart enough to discover.

However, if a customer buys some glasses or other fragile articles, you should wrap each of these items in newspaper—or tissue paper if the breakables are expensive pieces and you want to be extravagantly helpful. These paper-wrapped items can then be placed gently into an ordinary brown grocery bag or a small cardboard carton. You will want to start accumulating and saving these bags and cartons many weeks in advance of your sale.

It is also a good idea to have on hand some sturdy rubber

bands and some string to tie up such things as rolled-up posters, stacks of old magazines, or paperback books when purchased in quantity. Some small plastic bags into which you can toss small, inexpensive, unbreakable items also come in handy.

5. Am I better off selling only a few choice items or lots of stuff even if some of it is not worth very much?

Go for quantity. If you have only a few items on display, people will be on and off the premises in a couple of minutes. Not finding much to look at, they will disappear quickly, sometimes telling people they meet on the way in, "They don't have very much." On the other hand, a garage sale that has lots to offer the customer is more interesting and encourages the public to spend more time at your event. This, in turn, usually leads to increased sales.

It adds to the excitement of a sale if your merchandise covers a broad scale of prices—lots of inexpensive finds, certainly a few fine and highly desirable pieces, and plenty in between. In other words, something for every taste, every need and every pocketbook.

6. Do people expect to try out electrical appliances?

Yes, definitely. If you have a toaster, an iron, a hair dryer or a lamp for sale—anything at all that calls for an electric outlet, be certain that one is available in the garage or that you have an extension cord long enough to run it through a window to an inside outlet. I have yet to sell an electrical item when the buyer didn't want to make certain that it was operative. Actually, there was one exception when I had a very old nonworking iron to which I had affixed a tag reading "DOESN'T WORK. MAKES AN EXCELLENT DOORSTOP." It sold to a man who said, "I can fix any-thing electrical that's ever been made." He couldn't resist the challenge to his skills. And, obviously, he didn't think much of my doorstop suggestion.

7. I live on a main artery amid heavy traffic. How can cars park on the road?

You do have a problem, but it shouldn't deter you from running a garage sale if you want to. The advantage of living on a heavily traveled road is that hundreds of people who didn't know about your sale are tempted to stop if the atmosphere looks festive and there are cars lined up as far as the eye can see. One car will start the chain by pulling up half off the road, another will park behind it, and so on. I have seen garage sales attract impulse shoppers who had to take a five-minute walk. The string of cars made them feel they didn't want to miss out on whatever was happening.

If you're friendly with your neighbors, you might ask whether it would be OK for cars to park in their driveways, promising them that you will have someone in your family or a hired teenager stand guard on their property to assure that no one parks on the lawn or on otherwise forbidden turf. Don't, for pity's sake, let anyone park on a neighbor's property without first getting permission. Even big profits aren't worth the loss of a neighbor's goodwill.

8. What if it rains?

You have two choices. You can either list a rain date in your advertisement and flyer, or you can jam everything into your garage and go ahead with the sale as planned. Each alternative has advantages and disadvantages.

If you list a rain date, and that date falls on the weekend following the one you had planned, you will have to live with the merchandise stacked in the garage for another week; you will have to change any arrangements you may have made with friends who plan to help you (they may not be available the following weekend) and with any teenager, including the ones in your family, who had promised to cancel his or her own social or athletic activities in order to help you.

Of course, the advantages of a sunny day are good spirits,

leisurely browsing by customers, and plenty of walking-around room, and these pluses may seem enough to you to justify postponing the event.

Should you decide to go ahead with it regardless of the weather, and should this mean that everything is indoors, you are likely to find the premises quite crowded at times. Unless you have enough staff on hand to keep watch, this can sometimes lead to breakage.

The other side of the coin is that many people who might ordinarily be going to the beach or the golf course find themselves with nothing planned for a rainy day, which allows them plenty of time to stop and browse. If the rain isn't too heavy and unpleasant, you can sometimes draw as many people as in fair weather.

Of course, if it's a two-day activity, there is always tomorrow. The weather tomorrow might be magnificent.

9. How much of a budget should I allow?

Your principal expenses will be for newspaper advertising (except in apartment house sales where this item can be eliminated), tags, stationery for your flyers, and the cost of reproducing the flyer. Other items, such as old newspapers, grocery bags, cartons, and string, will either be available free or you will already have them at home. How much you spend on fabric to cover your display tables will depend on what you already have on hand or can borrow from friends and what sort of remnants you are able to pick up at a fabric store. If you plan to hire a teenager to handle car parking, which you will want to do only if you have a difficult parking situation, add that cost to your total, along with the cost of a permit if your town requires one.

Establish your budget by roughly calculating the above expenses. If your sale is to include antiques and furniture and is likely to yield many hundreds or even a few thousand dollars, don't be stingy. It will pay off if you are generous with your advertising budget. On the other hand, if your garage sale is to be a modest one, you can probably accomplish your objectives with fewer expenditures and more ingenuity.

10. I have had no experience at all in dealing with the public. Isn't it likely that I will handle people poorly?

Not at all. Even if you've never engaged in any retail activity, you've been a customer all your life, from the day you bought a piece of bubble gum as a child to the day you purchased your own home. *You* know what has pleased you and also what has irritated you in the behavior of people trying to sell you something. Just treat others as you would have liked others to treat you during those 10,000 or more buying transactions you've been involved in over the years. An inexperienced person has the advantage of not being jaded or bored with customers. You will do just fine.

19

How to Shop Someone Else's Sale

Now that you know what makes for a successful garage sale, you're going to be a much more sophisticated shopper when you pay a visit to someone else's sale. About the time you're planning your own, drop in on some others just to see what your local competition is doing in terms of merchandise, organization, and prices.

Aside from what you can learn at other people's sales, browsing through someone else's castaways can be fun. Even if you don't buy them, some items you will come across can provide a pleasurable trip through memory lane. Shirley Temple mugs, Mickey Mouse watches, Russell Wright dinner plates, an old Peter, Paul, and Mary record, a fringed piano shawl, a wooden washboard, trading cards, some Roy Rogers memorabilia—there is no end to the collectibles one can stumble across. The memories that can be evoked by such simple treasures can be delicious.

Apart from the fun and surprises that garage sales offer, and the simple fact that you might find something you would like to own, there's also the possibility that you will come across something that has been undervalued by the sale operator and is worth, to you, much more than the price being asked. When it comes to obtaining possessions, the greatest joy I can think of—next to getting something for nothing—is to get something for less than it is actually worth. All the world loves a bargain.

While your own common sense and gut feeling are all you really need to bring with you when you go browsing, there are a few tips I can pass along to you that will help you get the most out of your treasure hunting.

Shopping Early vs. Shopping Late

The obvious reason for going to someone else's garage sale early on the first day is that you get a crack at the most sought-after items, such as antiques, good secondhand furniture, and other merchandise that is currently in popular demand. If you wait until the end of the event, it's likely that the choice stuff will be gone.

However, you're going to pay for the privilege of getting first dibs. The early bird doesn't necessarily get the biggest bargains. The person running a sale almost always starts out optimistically, with healthy expectations about how quickly the goods will sell. Thus, the early hours do not provide you with the most strategic timing to request a price cut.

Conversely, an item, particularly a big-ticket item, that has not moved out by the final hours of the sale may begin to look like an albatross to its owner. If there is a real desire to unload it, the sale operator may well be amenable to cutting the original asking price. So, late in the sale is usually the time to get the best bargains. On the other hand, if you go early and see something you want but the price puts you off, you risk finding it gone when you return the next day to try to negotiate a last-minute price.

Haggling—and How to Do It

Bargaining at garage sales is not only acceptable, it's "in" with sophisticated buyers. After all, it isn't as though you are in an established retail store where the owner knows that he needs a 40 percent (or 50 percent or 100 percent) markup on the manufacturer's price in order to cover his overhead and other selling costs and still make a profit. At garage sales, prices have been determined on a very subjective basis and most people aren't wholly certain that their conclusion about the worth of a given object is necessarily correct. This uncertainty makes most sale operators somewhat flexible, which doesn't mean every price can be negotiated downward just for the asking.

Bargaining is an art—one that has been developed to a high art in some parts of the world, notably in the bazaars of the Casbah and among the street vendors in places like Tasco and Nairobi. To them, a potential customer's failure to initiate the haggling process takes all the fun out of the sale.

Proper bargaining requires two things on your part. First, you should know how much, or approximately how much, you would be willing to spend for the merchandise in question. Second, the art of bargaining calls for tact and graciousness. As the game advances, a small degree of toughness can creep into the act but, initially, you need to come on cool and courteous.

You won't make any progress at all by stating to your companion, sotto voce, "That price is ridiculous! She must be nuts if she thinks anyone's going to give her that much for it! I'd be willing to give her half, and even then it would be too much!" Or, "I've never seen such crazy prices at a garage sale! I'd be surprised if they manage to sell anything at all!"

No, that sort of approach isn't going to get you anywhere, except maybe *out*. The best opener is a simple nonaggressive statement of the truth: "I rather like this thingamajig and the price is probably very fair. But it's more than I would want to spend for it. Would you consider selling it for less?"

You will either get a flat-out "no" or, more likely, a response that asks how much you *would* be willing to pay for it. You can, of course, follow this by stating exactly how much you have in mind. But if it's a big-ticket item—let's say one involving more than $100—you can proceed by mentioning a price slightly below your true cutoff point. This gives the owner an opportunity to counter with a figure that is between her original price and the one you have stated. Should it turn out to be an amount you are willing to pay, the seller will be happy to receive more than you first offered; you will be happy to obtain the article at a price you consider fair, or maybe even a bargain. Happiness will prevail on both sides of the bargaining table.

The Leave-Behind Offer

Occasionally you will find an item you truly want, but not at the listed price. And the owner doesn't want to cut the price, either because she can't bear to part with the piece for less or because she believes someone else will come along who will be willing to give her what she's asking for it.

If you've come across such an item early in a sale, and if the owner hasn't responded with an absolute "No way!" to your request for a lower price, you might leave behind an offer to be considered should the piece go unsold by sale's end. "If you don't sell it, and you are willing to entertain a price of such-and-such," you can say to the proprietor, "here's my phone number. Call me and perhaps we can work something out." Obviously, you're not going to engage in this type of negotiation on some unimportant or low-priced article. The leave-behind offer is a technique reserved for big-deal merchandise.

Read the Ads

If you're in the market for some specific items—maybe furniture, golf clubs, a secondhand typewriter, children's clothing, a musical instrument, automobile tires, an antique clock, major appliances, a bicycle—comb the garage sale ads in your local newspaper and in the papers published in the surrounding communities. When you spot the item you are looking for, get to the sale just before the announced opening hour and try to be among the first people up the driveway. If you don't see the advertised item, ask for it quickly, look it over, and stay close to it until you have negotiated the purchase.

If you live in a small community and the sale is in your immediate neighborhood, you might even drive past the house the day before the sale, note the name and address, look the proprietor up in the phone book, and call to inquire about whether you could come around and look at the article before the sale begins. Naturally, if the ad reads, "No prior sales," you should assume it means what it says.

A Few More Words to the Wise . . .

Unless otherwise marked, a garage sale article (an appliance, shaver, lamp, etc.) is purchased on the assumption that it works. If you get home and it doesn't work, bring it back *during the hours advertised for the sale.* You should get your money back. You may *not,* if you wait until the event is over. So try out your purchase as soon as you get it home.

The largest selections are found in moving sales or estate liquidations. Where an entire household is being emptied out, you are going to find both volume and variety. Read the ads to search out such events.

Shop in affluent communities. Contrary to what you might think, not only do you find well-cared-for articles, but prices are usually lower in rich communities where people can afford to buy things new. In a less affluent town, where homemakers buy their large items secondhand in order to save money, demand for certain types of merchandise can drive up the garage sale prices.

Be decisive. If you like it and the price is right, buy the item when you see it. You may never see the likes of it again.

20

Laughing All the Way to the Bank

You may recall that in the beginning of this book I said some people, although not the majority, say they want to have a garage sale in order to have some fun. I also promised you that if you followed the advice in this book along with your own common sense, you would, indeed, be likely to have some fun while accomplishing your other garage sale objectives.

My family, friends, and clients enjoy telling about some of the humorous, bizarre, and strange things that have happened to us during such sales. And often when I address audiences on how to run a garage sale for fun and profit, they, too, seem to get a kick out of such stories. So, for no great purpose other than the fact that things are probably going to happen at *your* garage sale that will raise a few eyebrows and possibly amuse you, I would like to pass along some of these anecdotes. They may not teach you much more about such sales than you have already learned, but at least you will know that your own sale may be full of surprises.

Things—and People—Are Not Always What They Seem to Be

It was a Sunday morning in June, the last morning of a 2½-day sale I had been conducting. More than 75 percent of the merchandise was gone and I was busy marking down the prices on several items that hadn't moved, even though two customers had said they would think about some items and might return on Sunday. You should know that people who go to many garage sales often do this—they shop on the first day and return on the last day to see if the price on a particular item has been reduced. Of course, they risk losing the item to another shopper who wasn't put off by the original price. But that, too, is part of the game and garage sale hobbyists—those people who go to so many of these events that they couldn't possibly buy something at each one—not only understand the risk, but it seems to turn them on rather than turn them off.

To get on with my story, I had seen relatively few customers so far that morning, which didn't surprise me as people usually arrive much later on Sunday than on Saturday. Suddenly, a man on a motorcycle zoomed into my driveway, scattering gravel and scaring the hell out of my cat. Though the head of the driveway was blocked with one of our cars, he had skirted it to arrive on wheels. I figured it was probably going to be some thoughtless teenager, but as he removed his helmet and came closer, I saw that my caller was a man in his late fifties or early sixties, handsome, salt and pepper hair, with a nice friendly smile. He was wearing an old beat-up jacket and similarly disreputable boots.

After exchanging greetings (I said nothing about the sign out front that asked visitors to park on the road), he began to browse, ending at my headquarters station, a table on which I had a few pieces of jewelry. He picked up some of them, turned them over, put them back, and then casually asked, "You wouldn't by any chance have an old watch for sale, even if it doesn't work?" "Aha!" I thought. "Now I've got him pegged. He's some jewelry repairman looking for secondhand stuff that he can fix up and sell in order to make a few extra bucks."

I remembered that I had a couple of very old ladies' wristwatches tucked away in my dresser drawer. I hadn't worn either of them in ten or fifteen years and when I had found them during my presale rummage for merchandise, I figured nobody would buy a scratched old watch that didn't tick. If you can get a perfectly good, guaranteed Timex for under $20, why should anyone want to pay a jeweler to repair a piece of junk? So I hadn't put either of those timepieces into the sale. I told one of my assistants where the watches were and she brought them down. My motorcycling repairman looked them over carefully. One turned out to be a Longine in a gold case, but that was before the price of gold made history. I would, in those days, probably have thrown the watch away or given it to a small girl as a play watch without thinking twice about it.

"How much do you want for these?" asked my motorcyclist. I told him I didn't know, I hadn't given any thought to selling them but that he should make me an offer. He persisted in wanting me to name a figure. Finally I said, "OK, how about five dollars for the Longine and three for the other?" In a minute his hand was in his pocket and he was extracting $8 from his wallet.

"Do you have any men's watches you don't want?" He made the inquiry so casually he seemed almost disinterested in his own question. As he spoke he was examining a broken electric ice-crusher. I thought a bit. I knew that somewhere my husband, too, had a couple of nonworking watches that had been replaced by others. (Why do we hang on to watches that we will never bother to have fixed? I bet there are some in *your* house at this very moment.)

"What do you do with them?" I inquired, equally casual. "Oh," he replied, "it's sort of a hobby. I'm trying to learn how to fix watches." I didn't believe him, thinking he didn't want me to know the truth; namely, that fixing watches was his *business* and he was going to have a little more take-home pay if he could fix and sell my junk.

Leaving the sale area in the care of my number one assistant, I went upstairs and found not two, but three old watches that my husband hadn't worn in a decade. My motorcycle friend gave me $12 for the lot. Then, with a nice "thank you," he headed for his bike. I ran after him and asked him to walk his motorcycle to the road and he said, "Yes ma'am, I'll do that."

About fifteen minutes later, my neighbor two doors down, a man who had retired early after being chief executive officer of the largest advertising agency in the United States, arrived at my sale, walking alongside *his* motorcycle. We kissed hello and he asked, "Did my friend Paul Stewart (not his real name) come by on his motorcycle?" He described his friend, my customer, and I told him of the five watches I had sold him.

"Is he a jeweler?" I asked my neighbor. He put his head back and roared with laughter. "Paul," he told me, "is chairman of the board of one of the *Fortune* 500 companies. He earns more than $350,000 a year plus every fringe and perk you can conjure up. He may, in fact, be the richest guy you'll ever see in your garage!" He then went on to explain that Mr. Stewart had a theory about his wealth. He was convinced that inflation was going to get so bad that money was going to lose all its meaning. Therefore, he planned to leave his heirs various collectibles that would grow in value while the dollar declined. He was of the opinion that old watches would become collectors' items in time, which he did not mean as a pun. So he had taken a course in watch repair, just for the fun of it, and never passed a garage sale without buying all the broken watches he could get his hands on. My neighbor said that Mr. Stewart already had several hundred such watches, all of which were now in good working condition, thanks to his handiwork.

Mr. Stewart, I was told, also collected old pewter pieces before they came into vogue and grew expensive. And he had one of the largest collections of old radios, which he also repaired.

Well, I don't know whether Paul Stewart's theory about building collections instead of building a portfolio of stocks and bonds has any merit—that's not my field of expertise. But I do know that he is having a great time with his hobby, and that if he hadn't come along, I'd probably still be housing five useless watches.

When you run your own sale, be certain of one thing: when it comes to customers, you can't tell which ones have the money by the way they dress or by the vehicles they drive.

The Broken Hibachi

My family possessed an old hibachi that we could no longer use because one of the two iron pieces through which one slipped the grill section had been broken off. I taped the broken piece to the body of the hibachi and put it on sale for $3.50. I would have been happy to have someone cart it away for nothing just to get it out of the garage. It was unusable in its present condition and, to me, an eyesore. We placed it outdoors next to some of the junkier items that were for sale.

Suddenly, I heard what seemed to be an altercation. A man and woman were arguing and their voices were getting a bit loud. Walking over to see what the problem was, I saw that one participant was the man who services the pump in our basement. Mr. Lewis is a handy mechanic of sorts and it seemed that he wanted the hibachi because he was certain he could weld on the broken piece and end up with a large and otherwise excellent barbecue grill. The other customer was a woman, unknown to me, who was holding the grill piece of the hibachi in her hand. They turned to me to settle the dispute.

"I decided to take this," Mr. Lewis explained. "I even

moved it right over here with the other things I'm buying."

"I saw it first," said the lady. "I've been carrying around this grill for ten minutes just to show that I plan to buy it. I'm going to make a planter out of it for my terrace."

Neither customer seemed prepared to budge. I disliked being in the middle of their quarrel and I saw no way to resolve it. Mr. Lewis resolved it for me. "I'm prepared to give you five dollars for the hibachi," he said, taking his wallet out of his pocket to show he meant business.

At that, the lady replaced the grill on the ground. "I can get a better planter than that for five dollars," she said, and walked off. Mr. Lewis got his barbecue grill. And I, for the first time in garage sale history, got more money for an item than I had asked for.

Grass and the Green Stuff

Two young men I know were splitting up their ménage à deux because one had decided to move from the East Coast to the West. They had an eight-room house full of furniture and everything else that goes into making a house a home. They wanted to dispose of it all and split the proceeds. This meant that customers would have to go through the house to see the big furniture pieces in their natural habitat. It also meant that they needed quite a few friends to help as watchers. I agreed to lend them my services and alternated between handling the cash box and monitoring the comings and goings in the living room.

The event was well advertised and it drew large crowds from all the neighboring towns. By one o'clock, my friends had taken in more than $2,000 in cash and checks. As the success of their venture became apparent to them, they grew increasingly lighthearted. First a couple of beers made their way from the refrigerator (already sold, to be picked up the next day) to the command post. Later, standing in the living room talking to a potential customer, the unmistakable smell of grass assailed my nostrils. I soon found that both of the sale proprietors were more than a little high, as were two of their assistants. It looked like a great party was about to get under way.

As I mentioned earlier, I am opposed to mixing alcohol with cash handling. I am equally against the use of drugs during a garage sale, if for no other reason than it is illegal and you can suddenly find your place of business closed by the local cops. Even beyond that, grass and the green stuff you are taking in from customers just don't mix.

At about three o'clock I had a hurried visit in the living room from Charlie, one of the garage sale operators. He looked frenzied as well as stoned. "Do you have the cash box?" he asked. I didn't. He whispered to me, "It's gone. The box is gone. We can't find it anywhere!" I think my heart stood still. So much had gone into preparing this venture and both men needed the money to start furnishing their new residences. I got someone to take up my post in the living room and dragged Charlie into the bathroom. "When did you see it last? Who's been handling cash the last hour? Have you asked everyone else if they know where it is?" His answers weren't completely coherent but they did establish that everyone had been asked, no one knew where it was, and that Charlie, except for ten minutes or so when he went out to the garage with a customer interested in his snow thrower, had been guardian of the cash box. The staff concluded that someone had stolen the money while Charlie was away from his desk.

A great silence fell upon our group. The sadness was so intense you could feel it pass from individual to individual. Charlie said he was going upstairs to lie down. A couple of us combed every room, looked under sofa cushions and into cupboards, even into the refrigerator and dishwasher. No box. No money.

We went on with the sale. What else could we do? People continued to come and to buy, and we were making change from our own pockets. Charlie was still upstairs, perhaps asleep. Suddenly we heard a yell from the top of the staircase. Charlie was screaming incoherently and we thought he had lost his mind or was drunk. Then he came sliding down the banister, cash box in hand. We all left our posts and fell upon him. Where had it been? Where was it found? Tell us, tell us.

It seems that early in the afternoon Charlie had decided there was too much money sitting around the house and had taken the box upstairs and hidden it under the floorboards of the attic. And then, high on beer and pot, he completely forgot what he had done. It was only when he woke up from his nap that memory returned to him. We wanted to kiss him and hug him and hit him all at the same time. One of his more sensible and more sober friends relieved him of the money and drove to Charlie's bank, where he placed it in the night depository.

The next day, four of us announced that we wouldn't work that shift if anyone drank or smoked or sniffed anything stronger than tomato juice. But our warning was unnecessary. Charlie and his ex-roomy had learned their lesson. A boxful of dough needs a guardian who is as alert as a trained watchdog—unless, of course, you are doing the whole thing just for laughs.

If It Doesn't Work, It Doesn't Pay

In one of my sales I wanted to dispose of an old but very good black-and-white television set that we thought someone might like because it had a remote control. However, when we moved it down to the garage, plugged it in, and tried it, we were disappointed to find that the remote didn't work. This left us with a very ordinary, outdated, seventeen-inch (measured diagonally) black and white TV—not much of an article on which we could prosper. We put a price of $20 on it, thinking we would be glad to get that much for it. Had the remote control worked, we would have asked for $55.

An elderly gentleman picked up the remote, which was lying atop the cabinet, and said he was interested in the set. "The remote control doesn't work," I told him, "so you probably don't want it." He seemed genuinely disappointed. As he reached to put back the remote control gadget, he dropped it. As it hit the ground, the set suddenly went on. Like kicking an old appliance to get it to work, the fall had somehow corrected the problem. I picked up the control and pressed the various buttons—all of them worked. I turned it back to the elderly gent and he, too, played with the gadget. It worked. It seemed to be in perfect condition. But there was no way I could then raise the price.

"Take it," I told him. "It's all yours for $20." He was delighted. While my first reaction as I accepted the money was a slight feeling of disappointment, it was soon replaced with a warm glow at the thought that this poor old man (he was probably a good deal richer than I am) was getting such a fine set at such a good price.

Oh well, that's the way the cookie crumbles. And the way prices tumble when the merchandise is known to be out of order.

The Odds Are Against You

In disposing of the contents of an apartment, I wanted to be rid of a set of dinnerware. It had originally been service for twelve but I had only nine dinner plates left. I had ten salad plates and eleven cereal bowls, two of which had small chips. Having originally had some extra cups and saucers, I was now down to a neat dozen of each of those.

Because it was an excellent German china, I put the whole lot on sale, along with several matching service platters and bowls, for $40. It didn't sell. Although many people handled it, no one had made a move to buy it when we closed up shop at the end of day number one.

I had no intention of wrapping these many fragile pieces and carting them off to another of our residences, particularly since we were already well stocked with dinner sets. After some thought, I removed one dinner plate from the nine in the stack, took away two salad plates and three cereal bowls, among them the two that were chipped. I separated out the cups and saucers and put them on another table. I then printed a new sign: "SERVICE FOR EIGHT.

NO CRACKS OR CHIPS. PERFECT AS THE DAY THEY CAME FROM GERMANY. PRICE: $40."

The service for eight sold within the first hour of opening the next day and the couple that bought it seemed overjoyed with their bargain. The cups and saucers, twelve of each, had another new sign that read: "ONE DOZEN C/S FOR WHEN YOU HAVE GUESTS IN FOR COFFEE-AND." I put a price on those of $12. The same couple bought them.

The remaining bowls and plates were put among my junk-and-jumble items at 50¢ for the dinner plate and 25¢ for each of the other items. I priced the service pieces at $1.50 each. Everything went and my total take was $59.75. The first day I would have been happy to part with the lot for $40, which no one was eager to give me because it was a broken set.

Since that day, I have frequently used this device of turning service for twelve into service for ten or eight, always with excellent results. The same goes for glasses. It seems the odds are against your getting a good price for an odd lot. When you even things up, you come out ahead of the game.

The Giveaway of the Century—Almost

Stored in our attic for many years were three watercolors that didn't appeal to me and which I chose not to hang in the house. Someone in my husband's family had given them to him before we met and he had only a vague recollection of who the donor had been. He had been living in bachelor quarters at the time and someone probably thought he needed a bit of color on his walls.

One of the pieces was a depiction of many colored balloons flying in the sky. Another was a detailed reproduction of the George Washington Bridge in New York City, as seen from someone's apartment house window. The third was a still life showing two golden-haired ragdolls sitting on a table beside a vase of flowers. They were by the same artist. Each was signed "R. Naegele." They were dated 1939, 1940, and 1942.

Never having heard of R. Naegele and thinking that someone would probably like the balloons and the ragdolls for a small child's room, we put those two on sale for $10 each and put a $5 price marker on the George Washington Bridge.

At the end of the first day, none had sold and no one had expressed any interest in any of them. We figured they were even more worthless than we had thought. My husband marked down the prices of the bridge and the balloons to $2 each and put a $3 sticker on the ragdolls. They didn't sell.

Some people came to the sale with small children and I tried to interest them in the watercolors, mentioning that the frames were included in the prices. No takers. When the sale was over, I put the balloons and dolls into a carton in which I planned to start accumulating merchandise for my next sale. I offered the bridge to my sister-in-law who has a view of this monument from her window. I don't know why she would have wanted to be able to see the actual bridge and also have a picture of it in her living room, but she did, and to this day it hangs over her piano.

Several months later, my husband and I were at a dinner party when we ran into an acquaintance whom my husband had known several decades ago and hadn't seen since. This man, an art collector, happened to mention that he had just bought "another Naegele." We picked up our ears and heard him tell a small group of friends that Naegele had died recently after becoming quite famous in Germany from whence he had emigrated to the States in the late thirties. His family was trying to locate all of his oil paintings and watercolors so that they could compile an inventory of his work for the curator of the museum in Frankfurt, Germany, where some of his works now hang. My husband asked his old acquaintance what Naegele's paintings were worth. We were told that they were each worth many thousands of dollars, his watercolors a bit less.

The next day, we unwrapped the balloons and ragdolls and took photos of them. When the pictures were developed, we sent them to the German museum curator, advising him that we owned three Naegele watercolors (the G. W. Bridge was still in my sister-in-law's house) and asked him if they were of any value.

Imagine our pleasure and amazement when we were advised that, although the works could not be evaluated without actually seeing them, it could be estimated that the three were worth a total of several thousand dollars. The curator also supplied us with the name of an art gallery owner in Frankfurt who would be happy to auction them off for us should we choose to sell them.

If you had been at that garage sale, you could have had all three for $7! We plan to go to Germany the next time we are in Europe and arrange for our watercolors to be sold or auctioned. I consider myself a pretty smart cookie when it comes to garage sales, but I'm willing to admit I'm pretty dumb when it comes to judging works of art. If you have art for sale, your motto should not be caveat emptor, but *vendor* emptor—let the *seller* beware!

And here's one for the books: A woman at a garage sale in Wadsworth, Ohio, noticed a twenty-pound Bible with a price tag of $5. She bought it. Tucked inside the Bible was an old newspaper. Closer examination showed it to have a date on it of June 4, 1800. It was the issue of a weekly known as the *Ulster County* (New York) *Gazette,* and it carried George Washington's obituary! The type was hand-set and, according to the current owner of the *Ulster County Gazette,* there are only two other copies of that particular issue in existence, one in the Smithsonian Institution and one at the Massachusetts Historical Society in Boston. The value of the paper bought, cum Bible, by the Wadsworth, Ohio, browser turned out to be $25,000!

21

After the Sale Is Over

Your first big garage sale is finished.

You've closed the door on the public, folded the card tables, put away your props, tossed the draping sheets into the washing machine, and gathered your family and helpful friends around the dining room table to relax over a cold drink.

It's time to count the money. If you haven't yet done so, you now take your investment capital out of the kitty. And what's left is your profit—your rags turned into riches.

The big surprise of the evening is that you have probably made quite a bit more than you thought you would, even in your most optimistic fantasy.

Everyone at the table chuckles and guffaws over some of the funnier incidents that were part of the last few days' proceedings. They all talk about how the money should be spent. You, yourself, are feeling too spent to make any such major decisions.

What an Ego Trip It's Been!

Along with your exhaustion, you are simultaneously experiencing one of the best, natural highs you've ever known. *You did it! You* thought it through; *you* pulled it all together; *you* made it work! True, you may have had help from others, but *you* were the spark plug, the guiding light, the driving force, the one person without whom the whole thing would never have taken place. You proved that you understand people, that you have a talent for retailing, that you have organizational skills never before tapped.

If you're not feeling absolutely great about yourself at that moment, if you're not enjoying one of the best ego trips on record, then you're a rare exception to the legion of people who have come away from their garage sales with exactly such euphoria.

Planning the Next Sale

What better moment, then, to start thinking about your *next* sale?

True, there is practically no merchandise left, the new things you're going to buy with your well-gotten gains aren't going to be up for grabs for many years, and you haven't enough energy at the moment to put a rubber band around the dollar bills. But in a year or two! Next time, having learned so much from *this* event, what a double bonanza happening you can pull off! Maybe get rid of the den furniture . . . sell off the small rug in the guest room . . . switch from enamel-covered iron pots to stainless steel . . . and on, and on, and on.

And even if you don't see another sale in your own near future, why not offer your advice and services to one of your friends or relatives?

So don't discard the leftover tags, the old signs, the marking pencils, the money box. Save it all. Start collecting. Start with one sturdy carton, tucked away in the attic or basement. Every time you come across something you no longer want, every time you outgrow or outwear a garment, every time an appliance breaks and you decide to replace it, into the carton it goes, until suddenly, it dawns on you once again that the time has come to turn your unwanted things into cash . . .

. . . to turn your rags into riches!

22

Supplies: A Checklist of Things to Buy, Borrow, and Scrounge

Throughout these pages I've mentioned a number of items that you'll need during the course of preparing for and promoting your big event, along with certain materials that will be useful to have on hand while the sale is in progress.

In case you haven't taken notes along the way, here's a handy checklist of the principal props and pieces you will want to buy, borrow, scrounge, and stash until needed.

ashtray
bags, grocery
bags, plastic
board (or door to go across sawhorses)
boxes, cartons—small and large

cardboard for signs
card tables
clothing rack
electrical outlet

extension cord, if you have no outside electrical outlet

fabrics to cover tables
hammer
hangers
legal-size pad for inventory list
marking pen and sign crayons

masking tape
mirror
nails
newspapers for wrapping merchandise
pennants made from an old sheet

permit, if town requires one
picnic table
poles or sticks to hang pennants on
receipt pads
rubber bands

safety pins
sawhorses
sheet or drape for try-on area
staple gun
stationery for flyers

stickers, self-adhering
string
tags
thumbtacks
tissue paper for wrapping fine items

wheelbarrow

23

Schedule of Presale Activities

3 Weeks (or More) Before

- Check town rules regarding need for a permit or other local regulations.

- If required, obtain permit.

- Start saving grocery bags, cartons, shirt cardboards, and newspapers.

- Plan your staff for the sale. Talk to family and friends about helping out. If necessary, hire teenagers to distribute flyers house to house and/or handle parking.

- Systematically explore house or apartment, room by room and closet by closet, to locate suitable sale merchandise.

135

- Look over accumulated merchandise to determine approximately how many and what size tags you will need.

- Clean, polish, wash, and repair items whose appearance can be improved.

2 Weeks Before

- Write your advertisement.

- Make road signs.

- Prepare flyer and have it duplicated.

- Shop for tags, labels, string, receipt pads, safety pins, marking crayons, etc.

- Determine how many display counters (tables, sawhorses-cum-boards, etc.) you will have. Call friends and arrange to borrow some if you haven't enough.

- Buy, borrow, or improvise cloths and fabrics that you will use to cover display tables.

- Price and tag merchandise.

1 Week Before

- Make inventory list of all major items.

- Place ad in local paper.

- Distribute flyers to shops and post on bulletin boards around town.

- Call everyone who has promised to help you and remind them of the date.

3 Days Before

- Check newspapers to see that your ad is running as specified.

- Pick up borrowed tables, cloths, sawhorses, fabrics, etc.

- Distribute flyers house to house or apartment to apartment.

- Make pennants from old cloth or sheet.

2 Days Before

- Buy and/or make food dishes and snacks for the sale days.

- Put mirror in place and put up try-on curtain or drape.

- Drape tables.

- Rent a clothing rack.

- Start moving merchandise into garage.

- Check all merchandise and add price tags or stickers where missing. Check prices and alter those that seem too high or too low.

1 Day Before

- Put up road signs if weather is good.

- Set out breakfast items for next morning.

- Lay out clothes you plan to wear at sale.

- Go to bank and get enough money for opening day.

- Move remainder of merchandise into garage.

Early Morning of First Sale Day

- If day before was rainy and you could not put up road signs, do so this morning.

- Move display tables outside.

- Put merchandise outside, on tables, in driveway, etc.

- Put up pennants in front of house.

- Post signs outside your driveway and on premises.

- Put cash in cash box and take to checkout table.

- Eat something!

- Smile. You're in the public eye.

GOOD LUCK!

Index

LaVergne, TN USA
05 December 2009
166076LV00001B/38/A